Di

# Jersey

# Discover

# Jersey

## Terry Palmer

HERITAGE
HOUSE

**Discover Jersey**
First published May 1993
**ISBN** 1.85215.0394
**Typesetting** extrapolated in 8.5 on 9.5 Rockwell on Linotron
300 by Anglia Photoset, St Botolph St, Colchester, from in-house computer setting.
**Printed** by Colorcraft Ltd, Hong Kong.
**Published** by Heritage House (Publishers) Ltd, King's Rd,
Clacton-on-Sea, CO15 1BG.

©**Terry Palmer, 1993.**

    Titles in the 'Discover' series, in print or in preparation, include:
Discover Cyprus and North Cyprus
Discover The Dominican Republic
Discover Florida
Discover The Gambia
Discover Guernsey, Alderney, Sark
Discover Gibraltar
Discover The Grand Canyon State
Discover Hungary
Discover Jersey
Discover Malta
Discover Morocco
Discover Poland
Discover Sardinia
Discover Tunisia
Discover Seychelles
...and several of the English regions.

# CONTENTS

## MAPS

Terry Palmer (seen above on the Royal Jersey Golf Links) published his first guide book to the Channel Islands in 1977, and has been back many times since – coming by air, by car ferry, and even flying with the Royal Mail from Southend-on-Sea when he was press officer with the Post Office.

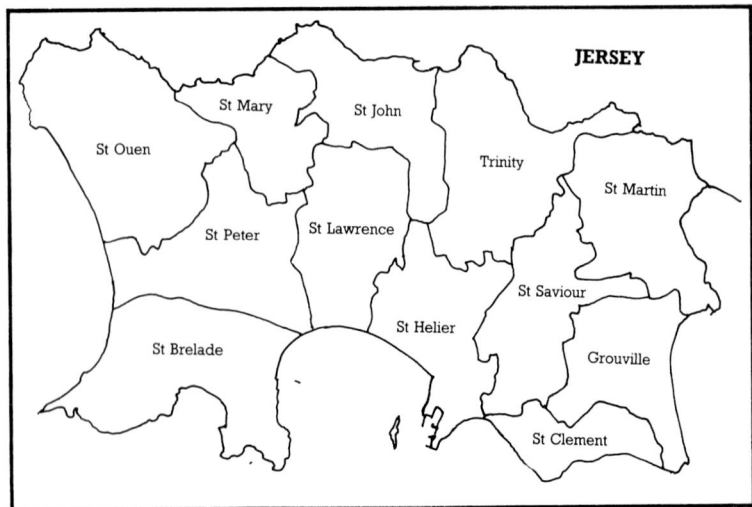

**JERSEY**

St Ouen

St Mary

St John

Trinity

St Martin

St Peter

St Lawrence

St Saviour

St Brelade

St Helier

Grouville

St Clement

# 1: WHY JERSEY?

## So different, yet so similar

JERSEY AND ITS SISTER-ISLANDS were never conquered by Britain. In fact, the reverse is true: the Channel Islands, as part of Normandy, conquered England in 1066. And since around 933 when Rollo added the islands to the Dukedom of Normandy, the inhabitants have been answerable only to the duke and his successors – with the present successor being the British Sovereign.

**How big?** Jersey is the largest of the Channel Islands, a granite outcrop covering 28,717 acres (44.87sq miles, 116.18sq km) with a population of 82,809 in 1989 (1,845 per sq mile, 712 per sq km). Guernsey is next in size with 15,654 acres (24.45sq miles, 63.33sq km), Alderney with 1,962 acres, and Sark with Brechou at 1,348 acres. Including the smaller islands, you have a land mass of 75 square miles (147sq km), one third the size of the Isle of Man but with twice as many people, and nearly half the size of the Isle of Wight. On a world scale, the Channel Islands would fit into Andorra twice, and the American state of Rhode Island 16 times.

**Potatoes.** For generations the island produced early potatoes and the celebrated Jersey milk for the British market, but in the 1930s tourism began as a serious, if small, business. Eventually, the island government's abolition of the 5% maximum on investment interest, and its determination to bring Income Tax down to 20% maximum and keep it there, interested companies and wealthy individuals looking for somewhere more welcoming that Britain with its sky-high post-war taxation. The stability of a government without political parties was an even greater inducement, and soon Jersey had become a major offshore banking zone, earning far more than it could by growing potatoes.

Guernsey had been involved in glasshouse growing since 1792, latterly with tomatoes, but it joined the financial and tourist industries as the horticultural market collapsed, although it still trails behind Jersey.

**Tourism and finance.** When the British government abolished currency exchange controls, much money flowed south to Jersey, and many companies moved their registered offices here. The island saw

*The Breton-style spire of St Mary's Chuch, once known as St Mary of the Burned Monastery.*

its future increasingly involved in finance, and drew up emergency plans to break free from monetary union with Britain if Westminster ever changed its attitude to this small sterling tax-haven. St Helier now has branches of Barclays, Lloyds, Midland, NatWest and the Royal Bank of Scotland, plus 32 others from as far afield as the USA and Hong Kong, employing around 3,000 people, some of them specialists from outside the island.

There is no tax of any kind on capital – no Capital Gains, Capital Transfer, Estate Duty or Inheritance Tax – and Income Tax, introduced in 1928, applies only on salaries currently above (for example) £18,000 a year for a couple with two children. The States is obliged to budget for a surplus, and now has reserves of hundreds of millions of pounds.

Tourism increased steadily, with 701,000 tourists staying at least one night in 1991, from 1,330,000 total arrivals, the others being residents, day trippers and business people. They more than filled the 25,000 guest beds of the original allocation some years ago. Tourism has much to offer: the unique history of the Channel Islands traced from prehistoric times to the German Occupation, all of it made familiar to British visitors by the long-running television series *Bergerac*.

Both industries have added to the heavy demand on housing, particularly as many hotel jobs are filled by Portuguese workers denied residency status.

**Houses.** The result is a two-tier housing market, with outsiders obliged to buy only in the 'open' list, where houses can be three or four times the price of identical properties in the 'local' list reserved for islanders. Jersey, being under more pressure than Guernsey, has restricted the number of immigrants to five a year, all of whom must pass the island's selection committee.

**Stamps and banknotes.** Since 1969 the bailiwicks have run their own postal services, although it meant the end of the private-enterprise Herm postage stamps. Jersey also issues its own currency, including the one-pound note, but British and Guernsey money is perfectly acceptable.

The islands have other attractions: they are very French while still being staunchly British, and English-speaking; they were the only parts of the British Empire to fall into Nazi hands during World War Two; and each is so very different in its own way without losing its Britishness.

**Taxes.** If you want further incentives, then consider that car hire in Jersey is among the cheapest in the world (psst! it's cheaper in Guernsey); petrol is almost half the British cost; and as the islands are not full members of the European Community none has Value Added Tax. Indeed, Sark's prices are so low that it has its own duty-free allowance for people going to Guernsey or Jersey.

**French islands.** But beware: some of the Channel Islands are French. The Iles Chausey returned to French rule with the Peace of Aix-la-Chapelle in 1668, and when the French claimed the Roches Douvres reef in 1869, Britain didn't contest it. The last territorial lines were drawn in 1953 when the International Court in The Hague decided that the Minquiers and Ecréhous reefs were British.

*Cows, potatoes and tomatoes formed the basis of the Channel Islands' fortunes before tourism and high finance.*

# The CHANNEL ISLANDS

**Casquets**   **Burhou**
Alderney

CHERBOURG

Bricquebec

Herm

GUERNSEY   Sark

Carteret
Portbail

**Les Ecréhou**

JERSEY

C O T E N T I N

Coutances

**Roches Douvres**

**Les Minquiers**

Hambye

*International boundary*

Paimpol

Gulf of St Malo

**Les Iles Chausey**
*(French)*   Granville

Avranches

Dinard   Mt St Michel
St
MALO

Dinan

# 2: CREAM and POTATO SALAD

## Facts and figures

JERSEY HAS ITS OWN GOVERNMENT, taxation system, and motoring laws. Visitors find the first two to be matters of interest, but if you're going to drive in Jersey you should know the basic rules of motoring.

## MOTORING

**Left.** Drive on the left, as in Britain. You can take your car to Jersey from Poole, and then go on to France, or you can hire a car on the island. From Jersey you can ship your car to Guernsey (worthwhile only if you stay for a week or so), but you cannot take it on excursions to Sark and Alderney even if you wish.

**Number plates.** Jersey motor registrations plates carry a simple J prefix, followed by up to five digits; all hire cars have a bold H on a white ground on the number plate, and the international plate is GBJ. Guernsey registrations are all figures, with GBG the international marker; if you see a car registered G11111, it's from Gibraltar. On Alderney the figures are prefixed by AY, and they're not needed on Sark.

**Seat belts.** Seat belt regulations apply as in Britain and most other European countries.

**Speed limits.** The maximum permitted speed is 40mph (64kph), with lesser limits of 30mph (48kph) and 20mph (32kph).

**Alcohol.** Jersey has the same laws as Britain on drink-driving, carrying a fine of up to £2,000, and you cannot hire a car if your licence has an endorsement for drunkenness within the past five years.

**Parking.** Parking is difficult in St Helier and not easy anywhere else. For the town you'll need to buy a book of **paycards,** each having a calendar and a clockface; scratch off the date and time of your arrival and don't overstay your welcome; limits range from 20 minutes to 6 hours. Paycards cost 20p, 60p and £1.20 and can be used in multiples, except when parking on the street; they're available on ferries, at the tourist office, from car hire companies, and in certain shops.

In quieter parts of St Helier you can use a **parking disc,** available at the town hall or free with your hire car; the Guernsey disc is also acceptable. Set it to show the time you parked, and move on before the end of your permitted stay, which ranges from two to six hours.

Paycards and discs are required Mon-Sat 0800-1700, and ♿ drivers must comply. The penalty is £20.

Parking is less difficult in rural areas, but Jersey has many narrow lanes, few of them with a pavement (sidewalk). Don't park where the road is edged with a single yellow line.

**Map.** You'll need a good map of the island, but even so don't be surprised if you get lost; fortunately, you'll seldom be more than a mile off course.

**Roads and road signs.** There are adequate road signs but most are, of necessity, small and therefore easier to miss. The main roads are all acceptably wide, and are classified A1 to A13; B-class roads may have tight corners, and C-class roads are narrow; on all the others, drive extra carefully.

Two road junctions give particular problems: the A1-A11 crossing at Bel Royal, and the A1-A2 intersection at First Tower. Here they are:

**BEL ROYAL**　　　　　　**FIRST TOWER**

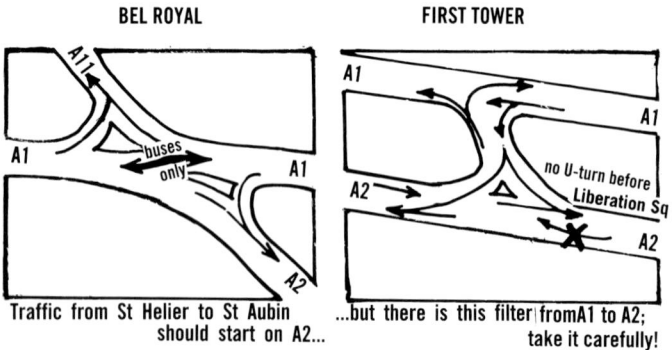

Traffic from St Helier to St Aubin should start on A2...

...but there is this filter from A1 to A2; take it carefully!

**Petrol.** Petrol is available throughout the island, with most service stations open into the evening. Prices are approximate: unleaded, 26p litre (£1.18 gallon); 4-star 29p litre (£1.30 gallon); diesel 24p litre (£1.10 gallon). Fuel is marginally dearer in Guernsey.

**Road signs.** A yellow line across your road indicates a junction with a priority road; a yellow arrow further back would have given you warning of the junction.

Several junctions have FILTER IN TURN painted on their approach roads; it's self-explanatory and means nobody has priority.

**Caravans.** Caravans and motorised caravans are not allowed on any of the islands – the reasons are obvious when you see the width of the roads. If you have a choice between a Jaguar and a Mini, leave the Jag at home.

**Car hire agencies.** Car hire is easy to arrange, but if you're doing it independently, give as much notice as possible, and check any age limits that may apply. This list is from the Jersey Tourist Board:

**A E,** St Martin's Garage, St Peter ✆54302
**A–Z Hire Cars,** 9a Esplanade, St Helier, ✆36557
**Aardvark Hire Cars,** Esplanade, St Helier ✆36558
**Avis Rent-a-Car,** St Peter's Garage, St Peter's ✆483288
**Barnes Hire Cars,** Victoria St, St Helier ✆21393
**Budget Rent-a-Car,** Airport Rd, St Brelade ✆46191
**Castle Cars,** 23 St Saviour's Rd, St Helier ✆23928
**Charles St Car Hire,** 14 Charles St, St Helier ✆21242
**Crown Garages Car Hire,** 9 Devonshire Pl, St Helier ✆24511
**Dolphin Travel,** 21 Gloucester St, St Helier ✆27727
*Doubleday Hire Cars, 19 Stopford Rd, St Helier ✆31505*
**Drivehire,** 17 Esplanade, St Helier ✆39222
**Eurodollar,** Airport Rd, St Brelade ✆43222
**Europcar,** Airport ✆43156
**Falles Hire Cars,** Longueville Rd, St Saviour ✆43222
**Fauvic Hire Cars,** Grouville ✆52540
**Gorey Hire Cars,** 33 Gloucester St, St Helier ✆33666
**Hallmark Cars,** 11 Caledonia Pl, St Helier ✆76122
**Harringtons Car Hire,** Rte des Genets, St Brelade ✆41363
**Hendun Cars,** 9 Lewis St, St Helier ✆79604
**Hertz Rent-a-Car,** Airport ✆45621
*Hireride, 1 St John's Rd, St Helier ✆31995*
**Ideal Hire Cars,** Janvrin Rd, St Helier ✆31995
*Kingslea Hire Cars, 70 Esplanade St Helier ✆24777*
**Leisure Drive,** St Aubin ✆43236
**Polar Self Drive,** Beaumont, St Peter ✆24577
**Premier Hire Cars,** D'Aubert's Garage, St Brelade's Bay ✆42283
**St Bernard's Hire Cars,** Carrefour-au-Clercq, St Saviour ✆56222
**Sovereign Cars,** 28 Esplanade St Helier ✆71238
**Urquart & Sons,** 63 Kensington Pl, St Helier ✆33340
**Viceroy Hire Cars,** 39 Commercial St, St Helier ✆26557
**West Park Cars,** Patriotic St, St Helier ✆26557
*Zebra Hire Cars, Esplanade St Helier ✆36556*

# CYCLE HIRE

Jersey is relatively easy for the cyclist, the main problem being other traffic on the narrow lanes. There are steep hills down to the bays on the north coast, at Gorey, St Brelade, and on roads down to St Ouen's Bay from the interior.

You can hire cycles at the car hire agencies *in italics,* and at:

**Good Health,** 79 New St, St Helier, ✆75057
**Lawrence de Gruchy,** 46 Don St, St Helier ✆72002
**Eastern Cycle Hire,** Gorey, ✆57024
**Roberts Garage,** Kensington Pl, St Helier ✆22481
ditto, Bel Royal ✆20644.

Good Health, Kingslea and Zebra hire mountain bikes.

In addition, **Ride Easy Cycle Tours** takes you to Grosnez Castle in the north-west and lets you cycle back to St Helier, downhill; ✆45873.

**On other islands.** Cycle hire is also available on Guernsey, Alderney and Sark; it is the best way to get around on Sark.

# MOPEDS

Mopeds, scooters and motor-cycles are available for hire; ask the tourist office for details. Drivers must have passed a test at least a year earlier, and it's a good idea to bring your helmet.

# BUS TRAVEL

Jersey Motor Transport operates the island's bus services, with every route starting and finishing at the terminus in St Helier's Liberation Square, originally called The Weighbridge. The schedule is designed for the tourist, with most of the attractions visited. Reading clockwise, the destinations are:

**Samarès Manor,** rte 18.
**Jersey Potteries, Gorey, St Catherine's Bay,** rtes 1 via A4, **1a** via Samarès Manor and A5, **1b** via A3.
**Hougue Bie, Zoo,** rte 3a.
**St Martin, Rozel Bay,** via A6, rte 3.
**Zoo,** rte 3a, with return via 3b.
**Orchid Farm, Bouley Bay,** via A8, rte 21.
**Jersey Pearl, Bonne Nuit Bay,** via A9, passing near the **Centre Stone,** rte 5.
**Retreat Farm, Butterfly Farm, Devil's Hole,** rte 7; from Retreat Farm to **Shire Horses, Grève de Lecq,** rte 7b.
**German Underground Hospital, Living Legend, Fantastic Gardens,** rte 8a.
**St Peter's Bunker, Motor Museum, Shire Horse Farm, Plémont,** via A1, A12, rte 9.

Glass Church, St Aubin, Lavender Farm, Airport, rte 15.
St Aubin, St Ouen's Bay, Jersey Gold, L'Etacq attractions, rte 12a.
St Aubin, Corbière, rte 12.
St Brelade's Bay, rte 14.

**Timetable.** Departures start shortly after 0900, the last buses back leaving at times from 1730 to 2359, to suit demand. Buy tickets for 1 day, 3 days or a week, allowing unlimited travel; ☎21201.

# OTHER TRAVEL

Seven coach companies operate excursions around the island, usually in association with tour operators, and you cån find *taxis* at the airport and in St Helier.

# INTER-ISLAND FERRIES

**From Britain.** British Channel Island Ferries runs the year-round car ferry from Poole to Guernsey and Jersey, but not to France. Reservations: ☎0202.681155. **Condor** has a high-speed car-carrying trimaran service from Weymouth to the two main islands, Mar-Nov. Reservations: ☎0305.761551.

**From France. Condor** links St Peter Port and St Helier with St Malo in France, Mar-Nov. Reservations in Jersey: 28 Conway St and Albert Quay, ☎76300. ☎726121. The French **Emeraude Ferries** takes cars year-round from Guernsey via Jersey to St Malo, and passengers by fast catamaran to Carteret, Granville, and Portbail on the Cotentin peninsula. Reservations in Jersey: ☎26452

**To France:** Day excursion with Twiga Travel (see below).

**To Guernsey:** Twice-daily (summer), daily (winter) car ferries with BCIF; four sailings daily (Apr-Sep) in Condor trimaran; with **Twiga Travel,** on a day excursion; ☎44229.

**To Sark:** With Twiga Travel, above; on Emeraud Lines' Trident catamaran, Apr-Sep, Mon-Sat; the cat continues to St Malo. There is no Sunday service to Sark from Jersey.

**To Herm:** There is no direct service to Herm as boats operate only from Guernsey; excursions from Jersey to Herm travel via St Peter Port.

**To Alderney:** By ferry to France then *either* go to Goury, near Cherbourg, and take the *Sea Fox* passenger ferry, *or* go to Cherbourg for the *Trondenes* car ferry – a long way around.

# TIDES

The high tide, surging in from the Atlantic on a front 130 miles (200km) wide between Cornwall and Brittany, meets the Cotentin peninsula and is suddenly funnelled into a gap 60 miles (100km) wide between Poole and Cherbourg. The result is the strongest tidal surge in Europe, exceeding that through the Strait of Gibraltar. The fastest currents of all, reaching 10 knots (16kmh) maximum, are The Swinge north-west of Alderney and The Race on the south-east, plainly visible if you fly into Alderney at the right state of the tide.

The **maximum tidal range** in St Helier, ignoring storm surges, is 30ft (9.2m) and it's worth noting that **spring tides,** the highest, associated with the new and the full moon, come around noon, GMT.

**Remember: holiday at full moon, high tide's at noon.**


# BEACHES

Jersey has some excellent beaches, with guards on duty daily 1000-1800 June-Sep at those marked ⇀. This listing starts at St Helier and goes clockwise:

**St Aubin's Bay,** the most easily accessible, with many free parking areas along the sea wall. As this is a curved beach, there are sections protected from all but a south-easterly wind. It's rocky between Elizabeth Castle and St Helier, and south of St Aubin, but the vast central area is ideal for building sandcastles, swimming and windsurfing. Toilets at West Park (near the seawater swimming pool), First Tower, Millbrook, Bel Royal, Beaumont (by the gunsite), and St Aubin.

**Portelet Bay,** a small beach protected by twin headlands. Free parking, café, toilets, but steps give only access.

**St Brelade's Bay,** ideal family sands, with car parking (fee) at west and at east, by Ouaisné ('way-nay'). Toilets in both car parks, ♿WC at west. ⇀

**St Ouen's Bay,** the largest beach in the islands. Usually has an onshore breeze, so ideal for surfing, and windsurfing in calm conditions; *but don't swim in heavy surf, nor at high tide when there is the risk of being swept onto the slipways and wall, or trapped.* Ample free parking; cafés and toilets at La Pulente (extreme south), Le Braye (south) and La Saline (north). ⇀

**Plémont,** also known as **Grève au Lanchon,** the first of the north coast beaches. Small beach, take care if swimming from rocks, and avoid swimming in heavy swell. Little parking, free, with café and toilets at top of steep path down to sands. ⇀

**Grève de Lecq,** by a small hamlet with ample free parking, cafés and toilets. Sandy beach shelves rapidly into deep water. Avoid the east side during heavy swell.

**Bonne Nuit Bay,** meaning 'Good Night,' yet not noted for sunsets. Limited free parking near hamlet at foot of steep hills. Jetty gives protection for children but beach shelves steeply into deep water. Café, toilet.

**Giffard Bay,** very difficult access; easier to admire it from La Crête

*The Jersey one-pound note has become smaller over the years, but has outlived its British counterpart.*

headland to west. Scenery impressive from here in afternoon as the Channel Islands' **highest point,** 446ft (135m), overlooks the bay.

**Bouley Bay,** pebbly beach protected from prevailing winds, but shelves steeply. Limited parking, café, toilet, access via steep, narrow lane.

**Rozel Bay,** tiny beach, but sandy and well-protected. Limited parking, cafés, toilet.

**Fliquet Bay,** tiny stretch of sand at north of bay. Parking and access difficult, and no services.

**St Catherine's Bay,** swimming only from the slipway at Gibraltar. Ample free parking; café, toilet.

**Havre de Fer,** south of Archirondel Tower. Limited parking and access to shingly beach, no services.

**Anne Port,** good sand and safe swimming, but limited parking and access. Good view from **Jeffrey's Leap,** 'La Saute de Geoffroy,' at south.

**Royal Bay of Grouville.** Continuous beach from Gorey to St Helier; from Gorey to Le Hurel the sands are ideal for children, with adequate parking places and toilets at Gorey Common. South of Le Hurel the low water mark is a long way from land and large areas of exposed rock may attract children: *beware being cut off by the incoming tide.*

**La Rocque,** Jersey's south-eastern point. The tide goes out more than a mile. *Beware letting children play in the rocks on the fast incoming tide.* Limited parking.

**St Clement's Bay,** good sands by the shoreline, thereafter large rock outcrops, to be avoided on incoming tide. Free parking at Le Hocq Point; toilets.

# AIR LINKS

Jersey has direct air links with 23 British towns and cities, and six on the continent, as well as with Guernsey and Alderney, the latter using **Aurigny Air Services,** Alderney's own airline and the only one to operate from the tiny airport, flying Britten-Norman Trislander aircraft with seating for 14 passengers.

# DISABLED VISITORS

Disabled visitors are welcome, including those confined to wheel-chairs, but there are limits on what can be done and seen.

The **impossible:** travel to Sark and Herm, as embarking and disembarking involves many steps; travel on the buses. The **difficult:** visiting Elizabeth Castle and Mont Orgueil, and some backstreets in St Helier; flying to Alderney – around one wheelchair may be carried per flight, subject to weight restrictions.

# COST OF LIVING

There is no Value Added Tax in the Channel Islands, and all other taxes are lower than in Britain and France – but there is the extra cost of freight for imported goods.

These are sample prices in Jersey:

| | |
|---|---|
| Martini Rosso 1.5 litres | £5.90 |
| Bell's extra special whisky, litre | £9.99 |
| Seagram's VO Canadian whisky, litre | £10.69 |
| Beefeater gin, litre | £10.32 |
| Captain Morgan rum, litre | £9.38 |
| Bacardi rum, litre | £9.95 |
| top brand cigarettes, 200 | £10.80–£11.10 |

These are sample prices on Sark, which has no direct taxation at all:

| | |
|---|---|
| Bucktrouts vodka, litre | £5.40 |
| – gin, litre | £5.60 |
| Bisquit cognac, 75cl | £9.50 |
| Lamb's Navy rum, 75cl | £9.50 |

Draw your own conclusions. The duty-free allowance from Sark is 20 cigarettes and 1 litre of spirits, but your full allowance applies if you are leaving the islands within 48 hours.

# MONEY and BANKS

The Bailiwick of Jersey issues its own currency, with notes of £1, £5, £10 and £20; there is no £50 note. Coinage is identical to that in Britain, but minted specially for the bailiwick. **The money is accepted throughout the islands, but nowhere else.**

**Banking hours.** Banks have the same business hours as in Britain –
0930-1530 – with a few staying open later. You'll find Barclays, Lloyds,
Midland and NatWest, and the Royal Bank of Scotland. You may also
see around 30 other banking houses including some from France,
Hong Kong, India, the Netherlands, Switzerland and the USA,
indicating how important the offshore banking business is to the
island's economy.

In 1834 Jersey changed from the *livre tournois* to the *livre sterling*,
at the rate of £1 = 26LT; all Jersey coins, since the first issue in 1841,
have carried the sovereign's head – but no Guernsey money has it.

# MISCELLANEOUS

**Phoning home.** The area code for Jersey is **0534,** which need not
be dialled for any numbers within the island. The code for Guernsey
is 0481. Jersey Telecom is, like Guernsey's service, self-contained and
independent, but is a partner with British Telecom.

To dial a British number, use only the area code and the number; to
dial a French number, prefix it with 010.33 (00.33 after April 1995)

Phone boxes give instructions in English, French, and occasionally
Portuguese, this last for the many migrant workers.

**Post Office.** The main post office is in Broad St, St Helier, with 22
sub-offices around the island. Jersey postage stamps must be used,
and the single-level tariff is cheaper than in Britain. Jersey introduced
postcodes in 1990.

**Dress.** Topless bathing is acceptable on public beaches, but is not
common. Shirts and shoes are required dress in most shops. Come
prepared for at least one rainy day.

**Electricity.** 240v AC, as in Britain. British plugs fit island sockets.

**Licensing hours.** Public houses may open between 0900 and 2300
Mon-Sat, and 1100-1300, 1630-2300 on Sunday. You must be 18 to be
served.

**Shopping hours.** Normally 0900-1730 Mon-Sat, but some close at
1230 on Thurs in winter. In St Helier many shops stay open until 2200
in summer.

**Climate.** Jersey usually has more sunshine hours than anywhere
else in Britain. The lines across show *average maximum* temperatures
in °F and °C, plus *average* sunshine hours; the columns headed **J, F,**
etc, indicate the months:

| J | F | M | A | M | Ju | Jy | A | S | O | N | D | |
|---|---|---|---|---|----|----|----|----|----|----|----|------|
| 46 | 47 | 50 | 55 | 61 | 66 | 69 | 69 | 66 | 60 | 53 | 49 | °F |
| 8 | 8 | 10 | 13 | 16 | 19 | 21 | 21 | 19 | 16 | 11 | 9 | °C |
| 65 | 89 | 148 | 196 | 247 | 254 | 256 | 234 | 174 | 130 | 74 | 57 | hours |

**Military service.** Channel Islanders are exempt from military service outside the islands, unless they are needed to rescue the Sovereign. They may volunteer.

**Public holidays.** As in Britain, plus 9 May, Liberation Day, marking the islands' emergence from German occupation. This is not celebrated in Alderney, which was completely evacuated.

**Religion.** Each of the 12 parishes has its own Protestant church, with the entire islands coming in the Diocese of Winchester, although the Catholic churches are part of the Diocese of Portsmouth.

**Tourist office.** Liberation Square (formerly The Weighbridge), St Helier, JE1 1BB, ✆78000; open daily, extended hours.

**Weights and measures.** The metric system is used, but miles and acres linger on. The *vergee* is an old measure of land, equalling 0.5 acre, 0.2ha.

# CALENDAR of EVENTS

Jersey has an active social life, but many of the events are carefully tailored towards the tourist industry. This is an *approximation* of what you may find, as the itinerary varies a little each year.

**April,** early, European Open Golf Tournament; late, Jazz Festival.

**Easter,** Hockey Festival.

**May,** early, International Air Rally; mid, Good Food Festival, *Salon Culinaire;* late, Italian Food Fair.

**June,** early, Portuguese Food Fair; mid, Irish Food Fair.

**July,** mid, Floral Island Festival; *Jeux Intervilles Jumelées,* games between twinned towns.

**August,** mid, Battle of Flowers.

**September,** mid, Battle of Britain Week; Folk and Blues Festival; late, into October, Festival France-Jersey.

**October,** late, Country Music Festival; Festival of Darts.

**Highlights from Guernsey.** Mid-June, St Peter Port Carnival; July, Harbour Carnival; Sark to Jersey rowing race; late August, Battle of Flowers.

# 3: THE CONSTITUTION

## And moving in

TO UNDERSTAND HOW THE ISLANDS ARE GOVERNED, it's essential to appreciate some of their history. They were a part of Normandy when its duke, Guillaume, conquered England in 1066 and became King William I as well as Duke of Normandy. But when King John 'Lackland' lost the mainland of Normandy to Philip II of France in 1204, the Channel Islands stayed loyal to the English Crown, which still symbolised the Normandy Dukedom.

In return, John granted them rights and privileges which, even in 1215, made them virtually self-governing, subject only to the Royal assent and enacted through the Privy Council.

The monarchy gradually lost much of its power in England to Parliament, but the Channel Islanders, like the Manxmen, remained loyal to their hereditary monarchy.

**Feudalism.** As England developed a parliamentary democracy, these little islands on the edge of France stayed in their feudal past. The manors – *fiefs,* pronounced 'fee-effs' – created by the Normans, survivied the pressures of change and are now the basis of the islands' governments. Sark is an excellent example as its sole manor has survived intact, and its Lord of the Manor, known as the *Seigneur,* is now the hereditary head of Europe's last truly feudal society.

Across the islands, those manors which fell into Crown ownership are known as *Fiefs de la Reine* (or *Roy* when the sovereign is a king): Jersey, for example, has such fiefs in all but two of its parishes.

**Warden.** The first ruler of the islands was a Warden, appointed by the English Crown. Early wardens were called 'Captain,' but as they gradually took on a military role they became 'Governor.' Later governors seldom bothered to take up residence in the islands, preferring to appoint their own Lieutenant-Governor, *lieu-tenant* being French for 'place-holding,' or the man-on-the-spot. Inevitably, the governorship faded out entirely.

**Royal Courts.** King John established a Royal Court to dispense justice, its chief officer or *Bailiff* (the word means 'official in a court of law' and is similar to the Scots 'bailie') being helped by 12 *jurats.* In

Norman French they were probably called *hommes juguers* but, like the modern 'jury,' the name comes from the Latin verb *jurare,* to swear, as on an oath.

The office of Bailiff, taking over from the Sénéschal of Normandy, gradually came to represent the civil authority, his territory being the *bailiwick.* Then, during the Wars of the Roses, beginning in 1455, the administration of the islands was split into two bailiwicks, Guernsey and Jersey – Sark was uninhabited and Alderney was leased privately from the Crown.

Gradually each island developed its own style of government, in Jersey the Bailiff and his jurats calling upon other islanders to give advice and opinions. After World War Two, senators replaced the jurats, and the States Assembly is now made up this way:

Bailiff (or his deputy) appointed by the Crown
12 Senators, elected by island-wide vote
12 *connétables,* (constables), one per parish
(non-uniformed part-time policemen)
28 Deputies (one from a small parish, 10 from St Helier)
Lieutenant-Governor
The Dean of Jersey
Attorney-General
Solicitor-General

The last four are Crown-appointed and have no vote.

*St Helier is not an old town, but it has some pleasing architecture: this is the NatWest Bank.*

The resulting body, the States of Jersey, is the government of the island in all matters except defence and diplomatic representation, which Britain handles. The States is not obliged to accept any law that Westminster may pass, but it frequently does so, often with some modification – for example, Jersey adopted Britain's drink-driving laws some years after they were established on the mainland.

**Privy Council.** The States is not the final arbiter, as all Bills must be submitted to the Privy Council for Royal Assent before they become law.

**Centeniers.** But that's not all. Each parish elects *centeniers* for purely local government, while its *connétables* collect parish taxes and, when needed, help the uniformed police constables in law enforcement: if a Jersey civilian demands to see your driving licence it's wise to oblige him as he may be a connétable.

# THE OTHER ISLANDS

**Guernsey.** In Guernsey, the **States of Deliberation** has a Bailiff, 12 *conseillers* who are Jersey senators by another name, 33 people's deputies, 10 douzaine repesentatives (there are only 10 parishes), the Procurer (attorney-general), the Comptroller (solicitor-general), and two representatives from Alderney. The **States of Election** has 12 jurats (magistrates), 10 rectors, 24 *douzeniers*, and two more people from Alderney. Together, these bodies form the **States of Guernsey.**

**Alderney.** Alderney was self-governing until the German occupation when almost everybody quit the island. In 1949 most of the government's duties were transferred to Guernsey, leaving an elected president and 12 elected jurats to fulfil purely local duties.

**Sark.** The feudal island of Sark is unique in the world for its form of government, the **Chief Pleas.** It's made up from the Seigneur (a hereditary title), an appointed **sénéschal,** 12 elected deputies, and all the *tenants.* When the island was colonised there were 40 tenants, but now the term applies to every property-owner on the island. If you buy one of those original 40 properties you immediately find yourself a member of the government!

**World's smallest country?** Depending upon how you define a country, Sark could qualify to be the world's smallest as it had, in 1984, 420 people on 1,358 acres (2.1sq miles, 5.4sq km). Based on area, the three smallest countries are the Vatican City (109 acres), Monaco, and Gibraltar (but The Rock's status is doubtful). Based on population, Pitcairn is smallest with 49 people (1990) and Tristan da Cunha next with 300 – but both are 'dependent territories' subject to Westminster, and Sark is not. Rule out St Pierre et Miquelon as it's considered part of France.

# FEUDALISM

Feudalism lingers on throughout the Channel Islands although it is less evident in Jersey. Until the early years of this century the seigneur of each fief received *congé*, 2% of the purchase price of all property sold. Certain property-owners were liable to pay *chef-rente*, a small tax on their homes, and *poulage*, originally two chickens but later converted to a nominal sum. *Quarantaine* used to be 40 eggs, but in 1927 this, too, was converted to a small cash sum as compensation for depriving the seigneur of the use of his land.

At one time the eleventh sheaf of all cereal crops was given to the seigneur as *tithe*, with farmers in a Crown-held fief having to give the twelfth sheaf to the Sovereign; the States took over resposibility for the latter due, and pay a nominal sum to the Crown each year.

*Varech*, the right of a seigneur with a coastal fief to claim all wrecks on his beach, has long gone, as has *escheat*, the seigneur's right to claim all property in his fief owned by people who die without making a will.

**Sark.** The first seigneur of Sark had the power of life or death over his subjects like a monarch of early Medieval times. He could claim each family's tenth child for his own labour; he could claim tithes on the fish catch until 1583; until recently he had a tithe on all corn and wool produced and the monopoly of milling corn, and he is the only person on Sark who may own a female dog and keep pigeons.

He is still entitled to the *treizième*, one-thirteenth of the selling price of property, and *escheat*, but the latter was last enforced in 1885.

# PERQUAGE

Since earliest Christian times, the islands' churches were sanctuaries for people facing arrest on no matter what charge; the Reformation ended the custom in the Channel Islands but it survived in England until the 17th cent. In Jersey and Guernsey the fugitive had a maximum of nine days in his sanctuary, after which there was no more food allowed in. His option was surrender – or to seek *perquage*, to follow a set path from the church to the shore, flee the island and never return. The paths were narrow and any deviation could result in the errant's arrest.

Several perquage routes on Jersey can still be traced, but not walked. **St Peter:** from the headwaters of a stream south of the church, to St Aubin; the airport runway cuts it, and the railway was in the lower valley. **St Lawrence:** west to the valley, then downstream to Goose Green Marsh. **St Ouen:** north-west to Ville au Bas and then west to the sea. **St Brelade:** the church is on the shore.

The **St John** perquage is uncertain, but probably involved finding the spring a few metres south of the church and following it across the island to Goose Green; it might have picked up **St Mary's** perquage near the Fantastic Gardens.

# THE CLAMEUR DE HARO

The most unusual and perhaps bizarre relic of feudalism is the *Clameur de Haro*, still used several times a year around the islands.

It's believed that Haro is a corruption of Rollo, the name of the Viking who created the Dukedom of Normandy and who added the Channel Islands to it around 933. Any of his subjects could appeal to him for help, and it is amazing to find that this appeal can invoke the power of the law more than 1,000 years later.

When an islander believes he or she is being wronged or cheated – for example, if a neighbour threatens his property – the appellant must kneel, hatless, at the site of the alleged offence, and in front of two witnesses shout: "Haro! Haro! Haro! A l'aide, mon Prince, on me fait tort!" – help me, my Prince, somebody's doing me an injustice!

In Guernsey and Alderney he must then recite the Lord's Prayer in French, while in Sark the entire clameur must be in French. The ancient law demands that the alleged threat or injustice must cease immediately until the grievance is settled in court.

*Hairpin bends on the C102 down to Bouley Bay.*

# THE PATOIS

Each island had its own version of Norman French, the *patois,* the two main islands having innumerable local variations. Until World War Two it was possible to tell from a Jerseyman's speech in which parish he was born; sometimes in which *part* of a parish. Nowadays you'll not hear the patois unless you go to evening classes, ask some of the older Jersey folk, or contact the *Société Jerseyaise,* which is struggling to keep the old Jèrrais alive. It's a sad fact that the local languages are not taught in schools.

Here's the National Anthem in Jèrrais:

> *Dgieu sauve not'Duchêsse,*
> *Longue vie à not'Duchêsse,*
> *Dgieu sauve la Reine!*
> *Rends-la victorieuse,*
> *Joyaiyeuse et glorieuse;*
> *Qu'ou règne sus nous heûtheuse,*
> *Dgieu sauve la Reine!*

Compare it with the Guernseyaise version:

> *Dyu sauve not'Gracieuse Royne,*
> *Vive, vive, not'Noblle Royne,*
> *Dyu sauve la Royne.*
> *Qu'a seit Victorieuse,*
> *Heureuse et Glorieuse,*
> *Long temps sus nous qu'a Raigne,*
> *Dyu sauve la Royne.*

This poem in Jèrrais was published in 1883:

### Les Consolations d'une Vieille Fille.

> *Nou s'moque des vieill' fill'; la! la! allez, allez!*
> *Il y-en a qui voudraient bien être desmarièz,*
> *Et se r'trouver libres et desenhalodès.*
> *Combein de fais j'ai ieu en memême du ji,*
> *D'les veîr haller lus llien, et pis v'nir ou pêpit*
> *Me dire: "Ous devriez voues marier Miss Hetty."*
> *Mais j'lus dis l'vier diton, erdit dans touos les temps,*
> *"Il y-en a pus d'mariès qu'i'n'y-en a de contents."*

Some words are identical to modern French, but others have strange spelling, such as *combein.* It is impossible to translate poetry literally and still make it rhyme, but this is a good English rendering:

Most Channel Island roads have French names, like this one near the Hougue Bie.

### Consolations of an Old Maid.
*You may laugh at old maids, but never you mind!*
*You needn't go far in the search e'er you find*
*Abundance of people in wedlock's grim chain*
*Who would just give their ears to be single again!*
*I soon take girls' measure, who say with a sneer,*
*"Miss Hetty, you ought to get married, my dear!"*
*And I quote them the proverb and slyly rejoice,*
*"There are many more married than pleased with their choice."*

## MOVING IN

Since the early 1960s and the development of the offshore financial services in the main islands, there has been a steady demand from outsiders for homes here, away from the clutches of tax inspectors in Britain and elsewhere.

**Two-tier housing market.** Jersey, like Guernsey, coped with the problem by creating a two-tier housing market; islanders buy in the 'local' market, in which prices are comparable with better-class homes in the south-east of England, but outsiders must trade solely in the 'open' market, holding around 2,000 larger properties whose prices are several times higher than they would be in the local sector. You could say the starting price is around £1,000,000.

Jersey folk can put their homes on the open market, subject to controls, but they are then compelled to stay in it, competing with expatriate millionaires; the only advantage is when they plan to move no more, leaving their assets to their children – tax free.

Until 1986 Jersey allowed up to 15 *rentiers* – wealthy immigrants – a year, but it's now down to a mere five, with competition having become very keen.

**J and K.** Workers essential to the top end of the island economy, which usually means skilled financiers, have to compete in the open market if they wish to buy rather than rent, while those serving the bottom end, such as catering staff from Portugal, have no option but to take lodgings: they may not rent or occupy property in their own name. The island's housing law states in Section 1 (1) K that an incomer may be admitted on social or economic reasons, hence the wealthy immigrant becomes a K resident, while J is the designation for somebody taking an essential job, such as a banker. The poor hotel worker never gets resident status.

**Selection committee.** The would-be K resident then has to gain the approval of a selection committee. No matter how rich he may be, he would stand no chance at all if he had a shady past, while people who have helped the island may exeptionally be granted their K even if they cannot fulfil the economic requirement – such as John Nettles, star of the TV series *Bergerac*, set in Jersey.

Other well-known incomers include television traveller Alan Whicker, writer Jack Higgins (real name Harry Patterson), cricketer John Edrich, racing driver Derek Warwick, pop singer Gilbert O'Sullivan, and Ron Hickman who invented the Workmate bench.

Cricket commentator John Arlott and 'Wombles' writer Elizabeth Beresford lived on Alderney; actor Oliver Reed lives in Guernsey, to where my industrialist cousin Haydn Coward, brother of Noel Coward, moved in 1975. No – not *that* Noel Coward.

# 4: CAECARIA'S STORY

## Stone Age to Duke Rollo

THE FIRST PEOPLE TO SETTLE in Jersey were probably Palaeolithic – Old Stone Age – people who wandered over the land bridge from France maybe 100,000 years ago, staying probably 50,000 years but leaving virtually no trace beyond their rubbish in the cave of **La Cotte de St Brelade,** on the south-east corner of St Brelade's Bay. Since 1910, archaeologists have found evidence suggesting at least 50,000 years of occupation in this cave, including 140,000 stone objects and vast amounts of mammoth and rhinoceros bone, making this the most important Old Stone Age site in the British Isles – much of which was later covered by ice.

As the ice melted and the seas rose, mankind moved away, probably leaving the island uninhabited for much of the next 40,000 years.

**Neolithic.** Around 5,000BC the New Stone Age culture arrived, probably coming up from Spain. These colonists may have reached Jersey on foot, crossing a marshy land bridge, herding their livestock but possibly having to float their precious grain stocks over the wettest parts: for these people were early farmers. But another 2,000 years passed before their descendants had boats strong enough to allow them to colonise Guernsey.

These new people cleared some of the forests for arable and pasture land, and for their villages. No trace of any of this survives, but there is evidence of their advanced culture in the burial chambers they built, first at **Le Pinacle,** (Pinnacle Rock), almost at Jersey's westernmost point, and at the extreme easternmost, now partly buried under Mont Orgueil. Remains of a third form the **Dolmen du Couperon** on the cliffs east of Rozel.

The Pinnacle, the most impressive site, is a mass of granite rising 203ft (62m) from the sea, sheltering a patch of ground where these peasants built a burial chamber from stone slabs; the site was in use until Roman times.

New Stone Age relics in Guernsey became the centre of late Medieval witchcraft cults, as the islanders felt the need to invent a reason for these peculiar stone formations; the best known is the

Grandmother of the Cemetery, a stone carving in the south-east of the island and revered until early in the 20th cent.

In Jersey, they created legends about their mysterious past, notably about Lady Hambye who is alleged to have built the Hougue Bie – but that's another story.

**Other relics.** Most of Jersey's other relics from prehistory lie around the north coast where they escaped the ravages of the plough. The **Hougue de Grosnez,** near the ruins of Grosnez Castle, is just a scattering of stones, and nothing but the site remains of the **Dolmen de Geonnais** 1.5 miles east. **Catel du Lecq,** east of Grève de Lecq, was an Iron-Age earth mound, now on private land, while north of St Mary, **La Hougue Mauger** was a Bronze Age mound holding funeral urns. There are tumuli a mile south-west of St John, just east of the Channel Islands' **highest point,** a 446ft (135m) plateau near a clifftop in Trinity; the earth fort of Le Catel north of Rozel, and the **Dolmen de Faldouet** near Mont Orgueil, where the 50ft (15m) passage and burial chamber had human skeletons when excavated in 1839. Here, too, the capping stone weighs 24 tons and was hauled from an outcrop 500m away.

The south of the island has yielded the **Dolmen du Mont Ubé** near Samarès Manor, an opened Bronze Age passage grave which, in an 1845 dig, yielded the only cremated and uncremated bodies in the same grave. Elsewhere there is the **White Menhir,** a small rock standing beside a lane leading up from Five Mile Road, and a

*Lillie Langtry, 1853-1929. The 'Jersey Lily' was aunt to a Viceroy of India.*

LILLIE LANGTRY
1853 - 1929

*'The Love Nest.' It makes a change from 'Chez Nous.'*

miscellany of odd standing stones. Perhaps the strangest discovery was in 1911, when 18 skeletons were found on **Green Island,** a high tide island off Jersey's southernmost tip.

**The Romans.** The Romans conquered Gaul in 56BC, scooping the Channel Islands into their net but scarcely bothering with them. They built a small fort at The Pinnacle, and another on Alderney, but their main legacy appears to be the naming of the main islands as *Caecarea, Sarnia* and *Riduna,* today known as Jersey, Guernsey and Alderney, the *–ey* ending, meaning 'island,' being a Viking addition. Additionally, three hoards of Roman coins, and a scattering of individual pieces, have come to light across the islands.

**Dark Ages.** The Dark Ages, following the collapse of the Roman Empire, were particularly dark in the Channel Islands. It is known that **St Helier,** the son of a Belgian nobleman, came to Jersey around 540, looking for solitude for his planned life as a hermit; legend claims he settled on the most inaccessible spot he could find, today's **Hermitage Rock** south of Elizabeth Castle, but this place had neither food, water, nor shelter. Pirates came in 555, allegedly curious about the gulls circling Helier's rock, and they beheaded him.

Around 555 **St Magloire** came to Sark, using the island as a base for sending friars to the other isles, and when he died in 587 his body was taken to Lihou (Guernsey) and on to Paris.

**Vikings.** History begins again around 814 with the coming of the Viking raiders, who seized footholds on the Seine and the Loire. In 911

Rollo, the chief of the Seine group, was powerful enough to take control of the Caen area from its Breton inhabitants and have it ceded to him by Charles the Simple of France at the Treaty of St Clair-sur-Epte. This was the beginning of the **Duchy of Normandy,** but it took Rollo's son, William Longsword, to add the Cotentin peninsula in 933, presumably including the Channel Islands. Traces of a Viking longhouse have been found at Cobo in Guernsey and in Old St, St Helier, but there was probably very little settlement. The main influences were the introduction of feudalism and of Norman law, *Le Grand Coutumier,* which was far ahead of its time and included the *Clameur de Haro.*

In the 10th cent, Normandy was ruled by a succession of colourful dukes: Richard I, the Fearless; Richard II, the Good; another Richard who was just III; Robert the Devil; and William II, the Bastard.

**Throne of England.** Bastard William had a good claim to the Throne of England as he was first cousin once removed to King Edward the Confessor, who had died earlier in 1066. Harold Godwineson took the throne by popular acclaim, but soon had to defend his realm against a Norse invasion, at the Battle of Stamford Bridge.

Duke William II saw his chance, and on 28 September he landed 8,000 men at Pevensey, Sussex, to claim the Crown of England. Sixteen days later he defeated Harold on what are now the grounds of Battle Abbey, and became King William I. Normandy, with the Channel Islands, had defeated England.

*This is the only French that you should learn for your visit to the Channel Islands.*

# 5: LES ILES NORMANDES

*"Morceaux de France."*

THE JOINT KINGDOM saw some anomalies in the Channel Islands, whose seigneurs paid their taxes to Rouen in Normandy, whose priests were appointed by the Bishop of Coutances, yet who were ruled from William's new capital, London. When William the Conqueror died in 1087, his elder sons split the territory, William Rufus taking the throne of England while Robert retained the dukedom of Normandy. Jersey stayed true to Normandy, while Guernsey kept its allegiance to England.

**Clameur.** There's an interesting anecdote to the Conqueror's burial. He was killed while attacking Mantes, down-Seine from Paris, and was to be buried at St Stephen's Abbey, which he had built in Caen. A freeman, whose house had been demolished to make way for the abbey, raised the *Clameur de Haro* for compensation, which was paid before the funeral could proceed.

**Treaty of Caen.** Four years later, William II and Duke Robert agreed at Caen that whoever survived the other should reunite the territories, but when William was killed in the New Forest by an unknown archer in 1100, the pair's younger brother Henry seized the throne of England. Henry I, 'the Lion of Justice,' had the support of the English nobility which allowed him to resist his brother Robert, who came back to claim the throne.

Henry proved his injustice by invading Normandy in 1104, defeating Robert at Tinchebrai (between Avranches and Caen) in 1106, and imprisoning him for his remaining 28 years. Jersey was back under the English Crown, while Henry continued his conquests, forcing Louis the Fat of France to surrender Brittany and Maine.

**Confusion.** Henry's son William was drowned in a shipwreck in 1120, believed to be on the **Casquets** reef west of Alderney. Henry therefore persuaded the Great Council to acknowledge his daughter Matilda as heir, but she, already the widow of the German emperor, married Geoffrey Plantagenet of Anjou and so reinforced the French complication.

When Henry died of a fever in Normandy, his nephew Stephen – son of William I's daughter Adela and the Count of Blois – urged the

Great Council to give the Crown of England to him rather than to Matilda, and in 1135 he became King Stephen.

Normandy, with the Normandy Isles, deserted Stephen and pledged loyalty to the true heir, Matilda, and to her husband, Geoffrey of Anjou. Now, Geoffrey and Matilda had a son, another Henry, who was not only heir to the Duchy of Normandy but also (because he married Eleanor of Aquitaine, the divorced wife of France's Louis VII) was the Sovereign of Aquitaine and Gascony: the total was more than half of modern France.

Stephen died of a heart attack at Dover in October 1154, having been forced to agree to Henry Plantagenet as his successor.

**Vast realms.** When Henry II succeeded to the English throne he had vast possessions, stretching from the Cheviot Hills to the Pyrenees, from Killarney to the Cevennes. And somewhere in the middle were the insignificant Normandy Isles.

Henry and Eleanor had seven children, the oldest dying in 1183. The thirdborn, Richard of Aquitaine, joined King Philip Augustus of France six years later in manoeuvring Henry's downfall; Henry escaped, but died of a fever in the Château de Chinon in 1189, leaving Richard of Aquitaine to become Richard I, the Lionheart. Richard spent only 10 months of his 10-year reign in England (see *Discover Cyprus* for his exploits in the Crusades), but his treachery was rewarded when the soldiers of Philip II of France shot him with an arrow.

**John Lackland.** Richard's brother John became king in 1199 – but all his French subjects except those in Normandy and Aquitaine preferred his nephew, Arthur. Philip II of France saw his opportunity and snatched Normandy from him in 1204, but never touched the Normandy Isles.

**Divided loyalty.** The islanders had a stark choice to make: should they remain loyal to the Crown of England, which still represented the Duchy of Normandy, or should they go with France? For most the decision was easy: England had the bigger fleet, and King John personally pledged that the islands' ancient laws and privileges would be maintained. But families who held land in the islands and in France had the worst choice, usually deciding to forfeit the smaller part of their estates.

The Iles Normandes therefore opted for the English Crown, where they have remained ever since, except for brief interludes under French and German occupation. The islanders' choosing to stay with England refutes any claims that the English conquered or colonised the islands, and makes them unique within the British Commonwealth. But henceforth they were to be known as Les Iles Anglo-Normandes.

**Enemy shores.** Work began on Jersey's defences almost at once with the creation of Gorey Castle, later to be known as **Mont Orgueil.**

*Herr Todt began his career by building German's* Autobahnen *but he rose to infamy with his slave armies in World War Two.*

There was little time to spare, for the first serious French raid came in 1214, and was repulsed. Henry III ordered that, even in quiet periods between raids, officers from Gorey Castle were not to spend more than eight consecutive days *in Normandy*. If the order seems unusual, we should not forget that Gorey was mostly manned by French-speaking islanders who would never have the chance to visit England, a foreign land which just happened to have the Duke of Normandy as its monarch.

Henry III followed John's example and came to Jersey in 1230 to reaffirm that the island's status would be unchanged.

**Jerbourg.** Edward III became king in 1327, after his father was murdered by having a red-hot poker thrust up his anus. The next year he recognised Robert the Bruce as King of Scotland, thereby worrying Channel Islanders who knew Scotland's main ally was France. Guernseymen asked Edward for a second castle and belatedly got Gyrbourg (Jerbourg), but the place was far from complete when the Hundred Years War began in 1338.

**Guernsey captured.** The Marshal of France, Sir Robert Bertram, seized Guernsey, Alderney and Sark almost at once. In retaliation, Edward III assumed the title of King of France with no hope of achieving it, and adopted the motto *Dieu et mon Droit*. In 1340 he defeated the real King of France at the Battle of Sluys (Netherlands), then sailed down-Channel and in August began the recapture of Guernsey. By October he had achieved it, except for Castle Cornet which held out for Philip VI for another five years.

The French took Guernsey again early in 1356, but their defeat at Poitiers in September led to the **Treaty of Calais** and their abandoning all claim to any of the islands. They would very soon render the treaty worthless.

Edward issued another Charter re-confirming the islands' customs and privileges, which every monarch has done down to the present, the sole exception being rulers who had no time, such as Lady Jane Grey who had the throne for just 13 days.

**Du Guesclin.** Let us digress for a moment. Bertrand du Guesclin, born at La Motte near Dinan around 1320, fought a famous duel with Sir Thomas Canterbury at the Siege of Rennes in 1356, and was rewarded by the Dauphin, who became Charles V in 1364. In that year du Guesclin had defeated Carlos II 'the Bad' of Navarra and in 1369 he helped Henry II of Trastamara to defeat Pedro the Cruel of Castille. By 1370 du Guesclin was Connétable de France, at the top of the military hierarchy and a man with a reputation to maintain; he wouldn't take risks.

So he waited until the French recaptured Brittany in 1373 before leading his invasion army into Jersey, and so scrapping the Treaty of Calais. He quickly conquered the entire island except for Gorey Castle which was still impregnable to anything less than heavy cannon, and they were not yet available.

Du Guesclin realised he was facing defeat so he returned to France while he could still claim victory: his minions would be blamed for not taking Gorey. A few weeks later the English fleet came to the rescue and drove the French out of Jersey. For withstanding the siege, Gorey Castle was given the name it bears today, **Mont Orgueil,** 'Mount Pride' (pronounced *mon-tor-guy*).

**Joan of Arc.** In 1415 Henry V defeated the French on a soggy October cornfield at Azincourt (Agincourt), a tiny village between Arras and Boulogne-sur-Mer, and once again took control of northern France – except Mont St Michel – thereby relieving for the moment the threat of attack on the Channel Islands. But three years later, in the village of Domrémy-la-Pucelle, Meuse, a girl was born who would change the fortunes of France. Jeanne d'Arc, believing God was her personal ally, drove the English from Orléans in 1429 but died on the stake before France could regain Normandy in 1450. Once more, the Iles Normandes stayed with England, which now held just Calais on the French mainland.

**Wars of the Roses.** Scarcely had the Hundred Years War with France ended in 1453, when the Wars of the Roses erupted in England (1455-86), putting Lancastrians against Yorkists.

**Royal treachery.** The Yorkist Edward IV (1461-83) was married to Margaret of Anjou, a French princess and a Lancastrian supporter. Margaret's allegiances understandably inclined a little towards her native land so that when she rewarded her cousin Pierre de Brézé, Compte de Maulevrier and Grand Sénéschal of France, for his help in her quandary over divided loyalties, she did it by *giving* him the entire Channel Islands, which he occupied forthwith as Lord of the Isles. It was the only time the French occupied Mount Pride.

The people of les Iles Anglo-Normandes, rightly fearing they would lose their independence under the French Crown, supported the Seigneur of St Ouen ('san wen'), Jersey, one Philippe de Carteret, who seized Mont Orgueil by a landward attack in 1468 after the English fleet under Sir Richard Harliston had blockaded it for five months.

**Grosnez Castle.** In this reconquest of Jersey, perhaps Grosnez Castle – 'big nose,' probably meaning the headland on which it stands – may have been one of the casualties: it's an oddity that nobody knows why and when it was built, nor who destroyed it.

**Bailiwick.** Liberated Jersey was created as a separate Bailiwick with Sir Richard Harliston as its first Governor; the title had earlier been Lord Keeper of the Isles. When the English freed Guernsey soon after, it became a second bailiwick, and it was from this moment that the islands began developing their distinctive political characters.

Mont Orgueil? Sir Richard reinforced it, adding the Harliston Tower to guard the main entrance.

**Papal Bull.** At the end of the Wars of the Roses, Edward IV and Louis XI of France resurrected the Treaty of Calais by agreeing that the Iles Anglo-Normandes should be neutral territory, and Pope Sixtus IV issued a Bull (a command) to that effect, which was displayed in the cathedrals of London, Canterbury, Salisbury, Nantes, St Pol de Léon, and Tréguier (both in Brittany), and St Peter Port church – but not in Jersey. The Bull proclaimed the islands and their waters 'as far as the sight of man goes' to be neutral in war, on pain of excommunication, and it remained official if not effective until 1689.

Despite the islands' owing allegiance to the English Crown, the Bishop of Coutances continued to appoint the parish priests until 1499, when Pope Alexander VI transferred the honour to Salisbury and later to Winchester, but in the following year the new rector of St Brelade, Jersey, made certain both bishops had authorised his appointment.

**Catholicism fades.** Henry VIII (1509-47) threatened the actions of both popes when he attacked Catholic principles by demanding a divorce from his queen Catherine of Aragon, which he effected in 1533. The Channel Islanders, who had seen many Huguenots fleeing from persecution in France and had listened to the ideas coming from Martin Luther, supported Henry and by 1547 had scrapped all outward evidence of their own Catholic faith: by 1560 the last of the wayside crosses, still typical of northern France, had gone, and the islanders were practising a sober Calvinist faith, with fun and laughter on Sunday punishable by a jail sentence.

**Sark and Alderney.** Elsewhere in the islands, Sark and Alderney had become irregular havens for pirates, until in 1549 the French Captain Bruel occupied uninhabited Sark with 400 troops and built several forts, but the men lost interest and gradually went home. Nine years later some Fleming adventurers seized the island and offered it to Mary I, who never replied. The disenchanted Flemings destroyed the forts and abandoned the unwanted island.

Unwanted? In 1565 Helier de Carteret, a Presbyterian Jerseyman from St Ouen, offered to recolonise Sark in the name of the new monarch Queen Elizabeth. She accepted.

**Elizabeth Castle.** In the later years of Elizabeth's reign, military men realised that Mont Orgueil was becoming vulnerable to the greater fire power of cannons. Their answer was to build another fortress in a safer position: on the rocky hump of Helier's Isle in St Aubin's Bay. By 1590 the military engineer Paul Ivy had taken over the project and in a decade produced a satisfactory fort, the new Elizabeth Castle.

**Sir Walter Raleigh.** As the 17th century dawned, Jersey received its most famous visitor, Sir Walter Raleigh, the new Governor for the new castle. Born about 48 years earlier near Exmouth, Raleigh had served a period in Parliament and a longer period in the Tower of London. He had also explored and named Virginia in North America, had sailed up the Orinoco and around Trinidad in South America. Now he had come to this castle named, like Virginia, in his Queen's honour. Unfortunately for him, he didn't stay long. Elizabeth died in March 1603 and her successor, James I, recalled Raleigh for a further 15 years in the Tower.

**English Civil War.** For generations past, Parliament had been gradually increasing its authority in England and Wales, although it still had no say in the Channel Islands. By the time Charles I was crowned in 1625 (1633 in Scotland), Parliament was too powerful for Royal comfort, and in 1642 the smouldering antagonism became the flames of civil war, eventually leading to Charles's execution in Whitehall on 30 January 1649. Meanwhile, with the monarchy under threat, where would Channel Islanders' loyalty lie?

Alderney had little choice as its Lieutenant-Governor was commander of a Parliamentary garrison. Sark's seigneur supported the monarchy. The people of Guernsey forgot their allegiance to the Crown and backed the Parliamentarians, except for the defenders of Castle Cornet. The English Lieutenant-Governor, Sir Peter Osborne, moved into the castle and defended it for the next eight years against Parliamentary attack until he was forced to surrended in 1658, the last person to haul down the standard of Charles I.

**Loyal defiance.** In Jersey, Sir Philippe de Carteret said "This island has nothing to do with Parliament, but only with the King in Council," and retired with his troops to hold **Elizabeth Castle,** on its island in St Aubin's Bay, while his wife Lady Elizabeth de Carteret took her contingent to hold Mont Orgueil, first allowing Sir George de Carteret, her husband's nephew and an officer of the *Royal* Navy, to gather sufficient ammunition for his small floating force. In 1651 Cromwell's troops invaded the island and began a long, slow siege of

*Gorey. One of Jersey's beauties.*

the two castles.

The political prisoner William Prynne, serving a sentence for publishing seditious libel, played cards with his chief jailer Lady de Carteret and wrote some verses, including:

> Mont Orgueil, which in scorn o' the Muses' law
> With no yoke-fellow word will daign to draw.
> Stubborn Mont Orgueil! 'Tis a work to make it
> Come into rhyme, more hard than 'twere to take it.

Prynne suffered cruelly, having both ears cut off, his face branded, and his assets stripped to pay a £10,000 fine. Times were not so gruelling for Sir Philippe, for when he fell seriously ill the besieging forces allowed him into St Helier town for medical aid, and when it was obvious he was dying Lady de Carteret was given free pass to leave Orgueil and visit him there.

One of the poignant legends of Jersey tells of how the garrison in Elizabeth Castle knew of Sir Philippe's death: his second-in-command played his telescope on a line of washing hanging in a garden in St Aubin and read the pre-arranged signal. In November of that year, 1643, nephew Sir George Carteret – he dropped the *de* – took command of Elizabeth Castle for the remainder of the siege.

**Royal beheading.** On 30 January 1649, Charles I was beheaded at Whitehall as a 'tyrant, traitor and murderer,' and Lord Protector Oliver Cromwell abolished the monarchy. The news took 18 days to reach

Jersey, but on 17 February 1649 Sir George, ignoring the *de facto* creation of the republic, became the first person to proclaim the succession of Charles II; the Scots were next.

Almost out of gratitude, the new king-without-a-kingdom came back from France and stayed in Elizabeth Castle for five months, still with his expensive and by now bedraggled entourage. Charles was so poor that Sir George paid all the Royal bills and was, in time, to be rewarded with appointment as Lieutenant-Governor and Bailiff of Jersey, Vice-Chamberlain of the Royal Household, a seat on the Privy Council, the Treasurership of the Royal Navy under Samuel Pepys, and a few islands off the coast of Virginia, New England. From James II he was to receive a much larger part of the American mainland, which he called **New Jersey.**

But that was later. Back in 1651 Cromwell sent Admiral Robert Blake to suppress this insolent Jerseyman. Blake landed his troops on the sands of St Ouen's Bay and on the next day, 21 October, at the **Battle of the Dunes,** Colonel Heane wiped out the Royalist resistance that had re-emerged. Five days later he took Mont Orgueil in a straight frontal attack, proving that the castle's military use was at an end.

**Surrender.** Heane then marched on Elizabeth Castle and, on a night in early November, had the luck to drop a 45lb (20.5kg) mortar from his lines at Mount Bingham, now Fort Regent, through a part of Elizabeth Castle's roof and down into the crypt, where it exploded, destroying 16 barrels of gunpowder and two years' food supplies. Five weeks later, Carteret surrendered to the Parliamentarians. Four days after that, on 19 December 1651, the defenders of Castle Cornet on Guernsey surrendered, the last people to acknowledge Royalist defeat.

**Major Peirson.** More than a century passed before Elizabeth Castle played its next – and its last – major role in history. One night in January 1781 the French adventurer Baron Philippe de Rullecourt sailed 26 ships towards La Rocque reefs at Jersey's southern tip. He disembarked 19 vessels and marched the troops to St Helier, arriving as dawn was breaking. Bluffing that 4,000 other Frenchmen were at strategic points in the island, he demanded the surrender of sleep-befuddled Lieutenant-Governor Moise Corbet despite being outnumbered six to one.

But 24-year-old Major Peirson of the 95th Regiment of Foot didn't surrender. Summoning the parish militia and five companies of the 95th, he seized Mount Bingham and advanced into the town centre. As he entered Market Square he was shot in the heart, but his troops fought on, killed de Rullecourt, and drove the Frenchmen back to their ships.

**Battle of Jersey.** It was only a small incident, but it has ingrained itself on folk memory as the Battle of Jersey. Peirson's watch is in the Jersey Museum and he and de Rullecourt lie in the town churchyard.

**Knitting.** After the Restoration, Jersey had entered a period of relative peace, broken only by de Rullecourt's attack. The fishermen discovered the Newfoundland Banks and their wealth of cod; other islanders expanded the knitting industry which had, allegedly, supplied the stockings that Mary Queen of Scots wore at her execution in 1587. A century later, the earnings from knitting were so great that men were neglecting the harvest to take up their needles. Britain's Industrial Revolution killed most of the trade, but knitted guernseys and jerseys still find a slot in the market.

The French were back in 1789, this time as refugees from their revolution. Many of the aristocracy settled in the islands, becoming loyal subjects of the British Crown and bequeathing a new influx of surnames as well as some of the smarter manor houses.

**Victor Hugo.** The French dramatist Victor Hugo who came to Jersey as an exile in 1852, later commented wrongly that the Channel Islands were *morceaux de France tombés à la mer et ramassés par l'Angleterre* – 'pieces of France fallen into the sea and gathered by England.'

**Fort Regent.** The troubles of 1781 as well as the French Revolution itself, reminded Jersey people that they were still open to a military threat from the French, despite having the two fortresses of Gorey and Elizabeth Castle. Plainly, something else was needed. Eventually John Hambly Humphrey of the Royal Engineers proposed another fort on the rocky prominence of Mount Bingham, also known as Mont de

*The manor at Puits de Léoville in St Ouen is typical of Jersey's rural architecture.*

la Ville, on the eastern edge of St Helier. After arguing over the amount of compensation, Britain paid £11,280 for the mount, then spent £375,203 on building the fortress, named Fort Regent from the Prince Regent, later to be George IV. The project was begun in 1806 and completed in 1814, only months before Wellington defeated Napoleon at Waterloo on 18 June 1815, so removing the French threat. The tops of the ramparts reach 175ft (53m) above sea level, and the well is 235ft (71m) deep. Some of the stouter walls are 18ft (5.5m) thick, and at one time there were more than 1,000 men engaged on the work.

The British never fired Fort Regent's guns in anger, so it was the Germans who hold that doubtful distinction, as they had an anti-aircraft post here. The British Army had evacuated the garrison in 1927 and abandoned the fort in 1932; Whitehall sold it to the States of Jersey in 1958, for £14,500.

**Martello towers?** During the building, General Sir George Don, the Lieutenant-Governor, had improved the island's roads to make troop movements much easier in the event of attack, giving better access to the round towers under his control. These towers had already been built on every lonely beach and in every small bay, from the northern tip of Guernsey to the low-tide rocks off southern Jersey, the oldest survivor being at **Grève de Lecq,** built in 1780.

Jersey got 23 of its planned 32 towers, most costing around £156 each and with a specification calling for a height of 33ft to 45ft (10-13m), the bottom 10ft being solid masonry. Designed to withstand yet another attack from France, they predated by a very few years the much larger towers that line the English coast from Suffolk to Sussex. As *they* were based on a structure built on Cape Mortella, Corsica, they came to be known as **martello towers,** and they're much more attractive than the gaunt concrete monstrosities built in the Channel Islands during the German Occupation in World War Two.

# 6: HITLER'S FORTRESS ISLES

## Die Ärmelkanalinseln

THE BRITISH GOVERNMENT, responsible for the defence of the Channel Islands, decided in 1925 that Jersey and Guernsey were so vulnerable to attack from France by air and sea that to defend them adequately may be impossible, and to defend them inadequately would be to expose the islanders to unnecessary attack. Therefore they would be demilitarised. British troops soon left Jersey, but they stayed in Guernsey until 1939.

By June 1940, with the Nazi *Wehrmacht* getting closer each day, Whitehall couldn't decide whether to uphold the 1925 decision or to send in troops. The two Lieutenant-Governors were appealing for arms: Jersey wanted two 4.7in (11.9cm) guns, four Bofors anti-aircraft guns and 12 Bren guns, not much to ask for – but the War Office while quoting a delivery date one year away, wanted £40,000 for the weaponry.

**Whitehall farce.** The lack of leadership and contradictory advice from London continued for several vital weeks, leaving the three States – including Alderney – having to look after themselves. As Hitler's troops drew nearer, States officials asked themselves whether they had been abandoned, or merely forgotten.

Finally, on 15 June 1940, Whitehall and Parliament decided that the islands would not be defended, and the Lieutenant-Governors, the last to go, left on 21 June. The civil evacuation, carried out amid panic, took off virtually every one of the 1,100 people on Alderney and 20,202 from the main islands, not counting those who travelled independently by mail boat. Only on Sark where Dame Sibyl Hathaway maintained feudal authority, did nobody opt for evacuation: the 471 people would stay.

With the evacuation and demilitarisation complete, one Government faction wanted to publicise the fact to prevent German bombing raids, but another wanted to suppress it as the Nazis would construe it as an invitation to invade.

**Invasion.** The *Luftwaffe* bombed both main islands on the 28th and the *Oberkommando der Wehrmacht,* the OKW, was ready for its elaborate invasion plans in which Stuka dive bombers and torpedo boats were to precede the main landing force of six batallions – but the entire operation was made obsolete on 30 June when the pilot of an observation plane landed on Guernsey's aerodrome and learned the truth: the islands were defenceless.

That evening, Junkers transport planes flew in a platoon of Luftwaffe soldiers and the occupation of Guernsey had begun. The following day, 1 July, was Jersey's turn, and hours later two planes landed on Alderney, cleared the barbed wire from the airstrip, and declared the island occupied. On 3 July a small detachment sailed from St Peter Port to Sark, and the occupation was complete, although none of the islands signed a formal declaration of surrender.

**'Anger.'** Britain had bungled the defence; it then proceeded to make matters worse by staging several commando-type operations, such as *Ambassador*, *Anger* and *Parker*, all aimed at Guernsey, which couldn't help the islanders and merely antagonised the Germans. *Operation Tomato*, planned to hit all the islands in September 1940, was cancelled. Nor was it practical for the civilian population to operate a resistance movement with organised sabotage, as there was nowhere to hide.

At first, life continued as before, with little interference. The States passed legislation, which had to be approved by the Kommandant instead of the King; church services and public entertainment were allowed; and it wasn't an offence to hear the British National Anthem on the radio.

**Insular life.** But soon problems began to appear. British markets for Jersey potatoes were lost, and unemployment became a major problem. Communication with the outside world was extremely difficult, and people needed a good reason for permission to travel between the main islands.

Hitler, meanwhile, had grand plans for the *Ärmelkanal Inseln*, the 'Sleeve Channel Islands.' While France would be governed by the French after the war (but under German supervision), the Channel Islands would never be handed back to a defeated Britain. They were to become outposts of the German Reich, providing holiday homes for the *Herrenvolk*.

But in the short term the Ärmelkanal Inseln, the first British territory to fall to the Wehrmacht, were to become the most heavily-defended section of the Atlantic Wall, although in practical terms they were more of a liability than an asset to the German war machine. Massive concrete gun emplacements went up at almost every headland, but the largest weapons were the four 305mm-bore (1ft exactly) naval guns at St Saviour, Guernsey, and camouflaged to look like houses; the underground barracks absorbed 45,000 cu m of concrete and had rooms for 400 men.

**Concrete.** Tunnels and concrete dominated the defences. By

January 1944, 484,000 cubic metres of concrete had been used in the islands, while the rest of Hitler's Atlantic Wall, stretching from north Germany to the Bay of Biscay, used 6,100,000 cu m. By the same date, 244,000 cu m of rock had been dug away, almost as much as the 255,000 cu m removed for the entire mainland part of the wall. To appreciate 484,000 cu m, imagine a solid block of concrete 78.5m (257ft) in every dimension.

The **Military Underground Hospital** in St Lawrence, Jersey, was dug by civilian slave labour, and involved cutting away 14,000 tons – 10,000 cu m – of rock.

**Land mines.** Hitler supplemented his concrete by laying land mines on the beaches: 67,000 in Jersey, 68,000 in Guernsey, 37,000 on Alderney and 4,500 on Sark. He compounded his megalomania on defence by having up to 37,000 troops permanently garrisonned on the islands guarding a civilian population of similar size.

Guernseyman Frank Stroobant recorded his experiences of occupation and deportation in *One Man's War,* a story which could equally have applied to Jersey. Stroobant's first act of defiance was his serving of condemned meat to German troops in his harbourside restaurant. When cooking fat vanished from the market he nearly gassed himself by frying chips in linseed oil, having decided that motor oil was too dangerous. Stroobant found a publisher, the Guernsey Press, in 1967, and his book has been in print ever since.

Stroobant comments that the Germans at first believed the islanders to be unwilling subjects of British colonialism, but changed their opinion after the loss of HMS *Charybdis* early in the war. When the Germans held a military funeral for the 19 British bodies washed ashore, 'scarcely an islander was absent from the service' and 721 wreaths were sent.

*Noirmont Point offers wonderful views to St Helier, so the Germans had to put a gun there. It's now a part of history.*

The various museums show the more serious side of life under occupation, such an the epitaph to *Louis Berrier, charged with having released a pigeon with a message for England. He was therefore sentenced to death for espionage by the Court Martial and shot on 2nd August 1941*. Usually the islanders had no option but passive resistance, such as by painting BRITISH VICTORY IS CERTAIN on road signs. The Germans countered this by painting their own 'V' signs, although the German for 'victory' is *Sieg*.

**Food shortages.** Gradually and relentlessly, hunger began to rule people's lives, especially after the Allies' invasion of Normandy in 1944, which cut off all supplies from France. The islanders roasted and crushed lupin seeds, acorns, parsnips and sugar beet in their search for a coffee substitute; parsnips, pea pods, bramble leaves and carrots served for tea; dried elderberries became sultanas; coltsfoot, bramble, and sweet chestnut leaves served as tobacco; and potatoes were milled for flour. The Germans imposed stringent restrictions on fishing, leading to yet another substitute: macaroni and anchovy sauce boiled until stiff, then fried. It made a ghastly fish dish.

In the final days even the Germans were near starvation, as shown by the last menu for the garrison in Elizabeth Castle:

*Morgen: 100gm Brot.*
*Mittag: Suppe Nudeln; Goulasch.*
*Abend: Eintopf; Wurst, 80gm; Butter, 35gm; Kaffee; Brot.*

Morning: 3.7oz bread.
Midday: Noodle soup, goulash.
Evening: Stew, 2.75oz sausage, 1.25oz butter, coffee, bread.

**Black market.** Midway through the war, most shops were open for only a few hours daily but, beyond the business centres, the black market was in operation, with goods being sold for British money, not the unpopular Occupation Reichsmarks. Butter cost £2 a pound (90p kg) and meat was 15/– a pound (34p kg), at a time when £3 was a good weekly wage. Eggs were 2/– (10p) each, a hundredweight (50kg) of wheat was worth £25, and a farm horse sold for £500.

The 319th German Infantry Division which came in 1941 brought more than 600 horses, mostly taken from French farms. After the Normandy landings the 4oz (113gm) weekly meat ration ceased, and soon civilians and soldiers alike were eating the horses; only 308 were left when the islands were liberated. They were sold to the farmers, the last one dying in 1968.

**Bureaucracy.** To prevent the troops joining the black market, every purchase had to be backed by a licence from the *Feldkommandantur*, even for one shirt button, until the Germans realised the stupidity of such an order. At another time, all boats in Jersey had to be taken to St Helier at short notice: it wasn't enough to report their existence. The order included everything that was capable of floating, including canoes and fishing boats that had been laid up with their engines taken out.

**Escapes.** Only one person escaped from the islands, the notorious Channel currents perhaps being a main deterrent. Denis Vibert's first attempt stranded him on Les Roches Douvres, reefs 20 miles (32km) west of Corbière, from where he was washed back to Jersey four days later. On his second journey in 1941 in a 9ft (2.75m) open boat from St Aubin's Bay, Jersey, he took three days to reach a minefield off Portland Bill, where the British picked him up. His boat is on display in the Hougue Bie Museum.

**Deportation.** The greatest exodus of civilians came in 1942 when 1,182 British-born islanders were deported to Germany, many at only a day's notice. A year earlier, Britain had asked that German residents in Iran should be handed over; Hitler's response was to demand British residents in the Channel Islands be sent to Germany – but on a ten-for-one basis. The order was quietly forgotten until the Swiss Government suggested an exchange of wounded prisoners, and Hitler remembered this deportation.

**Organization Todt.** The transported Britons received reasonable treatment, as far as life in a concentration camp can be considered reasonable, but back in the Channel Islands several thousand Organization Todt workers were cruelly abused. Dr Fritz Todt had devised his bestial organisation before the war, and now he used it to bring in starving survivors of the Spanish Civil War, French Jews, plus Ukrainians who, allegedly, walked barefoot across Europe, and others who had become dregs of humanity. It was coincidence that *Tod* is German for 'death,' but eyewitness accounts claim that hundreds, if not thousands, of OT workers starved to death or were murdered – although hard proof is difficult to establish.

**Concentration camp.** Solomon Steckoll claimed in his book *The Alderney Death Camp* (Granada, 1982) that of the four camps for slave labourers on Alderney, the one called Sylt, beside the airport runway, was as much an extermination camp as Dachau, Sachsenhausen and Belsen, although it lacked gas chambers and incinerators. The notorious SS – *Schutzstaffel*, 'protection squad' – whose officers guarded Sylt, had some very special German prisoners under their control: 120 *Wehrmacht* ('Army') and two SS officers, many of whom had been decorated by Hitler in person, but who had been convicted of treason and were awaiting 'special punishment' after the war. Major-General Count Rudolf von Schmettow, the Kommandant of the occupied islands, confirmed up to 3,000 OT workers were on Alderney in 1943, and 13,000 were elsewhere, and it is on record that the entire Organization Todt was withdrawn soon after the Normandy landings, as there was no further point in building concrete bunkers. But Steckoll insists there was a major cover-up after the war to prevent news of Sylt leaking to the public.

**Bypassed.** Meanwhile, Operation Overlord, the invasion of Europe, bypassed the Channel Islands for several reasons: the manpower and materiel necessary for their liberation would be too much; there would be major damage to property; the islands were not strategic; and the islanders were on reasonable terms with the occupiers.

**Starvation.** As the last winter of the war approached, and the Allies headed for Paris and the Rhine, some high-ranking German officers tried to persusade Hitler to evacuate all Channel Island civilians to France. After the German loss of St Malo this changed to appeals to ask the British to evacuate the islanders, or to send them food. The British Government approved the mercy rations but Prime Minister Winston Churchill refused to risk British food going to any of the 28,500 German troops instead of to the 62,000 remaining islanders.

"Let 'em starve," he wrote. "No fighting. They can rot at their leisure." He meant the Wehrmacht but, as Germany would not surrender the Ärmelkanal Inseln, his comments applied to all 90,500 people.

**Surrender.** Adolf Hitler's death was announced on 1 May, 1945, heralding the German surrender. On 8 May Churchill had the more comforting words "...and our dear Channel Islands will be freed today," but it was early on 9 May when the Royal Navy entered St Peter Port, and a few hours later when Jersey was officially free. Peace was two days old before British troops managed to reach Sark, and Alderney was liberated on 16 May, the very last German outpost to surrender. The war in Europe was at an end.

For a full account read *The German Occupation of the Channel Islands*, by Dr Charles Cruikshank, published by the Guernsey Press and continually in print.

*St Ouen's Bay from the south on a mirror-calm day in August (above);
Grève de Lecq beach is much smaller and fills up quickly.*

*Bonne Nuit Bay (above), with the Cheval de Guillaume almost covered by the high tide; below, Lillie Langtry's lily-white bust graces St Saviour's churchyard.*

# 7: ISLES OF LEGEND

## Little islands; little folk

BEWARE TCHICO; he's evil. Tchico is a spectral dog, quite often black but sometimes invisible save for his big, staring eyes. He roams the islands by night and is a warning of bad news to come. The strange thing is that the legend of Tchico, the dog with big eyes, is found in many places in Britain, where he's called Black Shuck, and to a lesser degree in France; there's even a Sarkese Tchico who wanders across La Coupée, the causeway to Little Sark.

**Chevauchage.** In feudal times the peasants had their bonds of allegiance relaxed for one day a year, when they ran around the parishes kissing every female they saw, even if she were the seigneur's own wife.

Various seigneurs at various times held extraordinary power over their serfs, such as the right to take to bed any young woman they

*The Dolmen de Faldouet, excavated in 1839, has an exposed passage grave 15m long.*

fancied. Most seigneurs whose fiefs ran down to the beach had the right to claim all wreckage, and an unknown number have lit large fires on dangerous coasts on stormy nights – not to serve as warnings, but to infer the safety of a harbour.

**Witchcraft.** Belief in witches and witchcraft in the Middle Ages was rife in the islands, as indeed it was in England and France.

In the early 1880s a man from St Saviour wanting to rid himself of his late father's *mauvais livres,* 'bad books' containing spells, threw them on the fire. They put the flames out. He dropped them down a well; it dried up. Finally, on advice, he buried them in their own element at the bottom of a pile of farmyard manure, where the ammonia destroyed them.

In Jersey, witches are supposed to have danced naked at their sabbats at La Rocqueberg, and cast spells on passing fishermen to induce them to join in.

**Fairies...** But Jersey has even better tales of fairies and monsters. Take, for example, **La Table des Marthes,** the 'Martys's Table,' which the little folk, *les p'tits faitiaux,* brought to this site on Corbière beside where the railway station would later be built.

**...and ghosts.** Among the hundreds of ghost stories about Jersey is the simple tale of the Pierres de Lecq, rocks two miles (3km) north of Grève de Lecq. According to legend, in 1565 Helier de Carteret, Seigneur of St Ouen, sailing to colonise Sark, lost a ship on these rocks. For evermore, the drowned children aboard the ship cry out to

*The Martyr's Table near Corbière. People now walk where the trains once trundled by.*

warn of approaching storms, the sound often heard in Grève de Lecq itself. Passing fishermen began saying a pater noster when passing the rocks, which are now known as the **Paternoster Rocks.**

A bride, abandoned by her husband-to-be outside St Lawrence Church, still searches for him in her wedding coach whenever the bells ring for a marriage.

**The Lord of Hambye.** The **Hougue Bie** is one of the largest burial chambers that the Beaker Folk built anywhere; it has 53 massive stones forming the walls with 17 in the ceiling, and even now it's an eerie experience to shuffle along the chest-high passage to those tombs built in prehistoric times. 'Hougue' comes from *Haugr,* the Old Norse for 'hillock,'and 'Bie' soon becomes obvious.

Folklore has another explanation for this man-made hillock. Once upon a proverbial time there lived in the Goose Green Marsh of Jersey a fearsome dragon which terrorised the locals. In the little town of Hambye, between Granville and St Lô, there lived a brave knight, the Lord of Hambye, who crossed to Jersey and slew the dragon, after which he lay down to rest.

His servant then murdered him, buried the body, and went back to Hambye to tell the lady that the dragon had slain her husband. She was so distraught that she accepted the manservant's next lie, that the lord's dying wish was that she marry *him.*Trouble came when the newlywed underling talked in his sleep and condemned himself, for which he was hanged. The Lady Hambye then went to Jersey and had a large mound built over her husband's grave, and she called it La Hougue Hambye.

The local version of the story is vague on why she chose St Saviour when Goose Green (and, presumably, the scene of the murder) is in Sts Peter and Lawrence, but the French version claims it was to allow her to see the grave marker from her castle at Hambye. And the ruins of this castle exist to this day.

Fact and fiction have another curious link in that a descendant of the seigneur of Hambye became a seigneur of St Clement, but *his* descendant forfeited his Jersey fief in 1204 when the islands were detached politically from Normandy.

The island version of the legend of Hambye was recorded in the manuscripts of Sir Philippe de Carteret, defender of Elizabeth Castle in the English Civil War. A female ancestor of this de Carteret had married the 16th-cent bailiff George Paulet and *his* grim claim to fame was that he ordered the execution of 18 women for witchcraft. There are no such executions today, but many visitors still find the island bewitching.

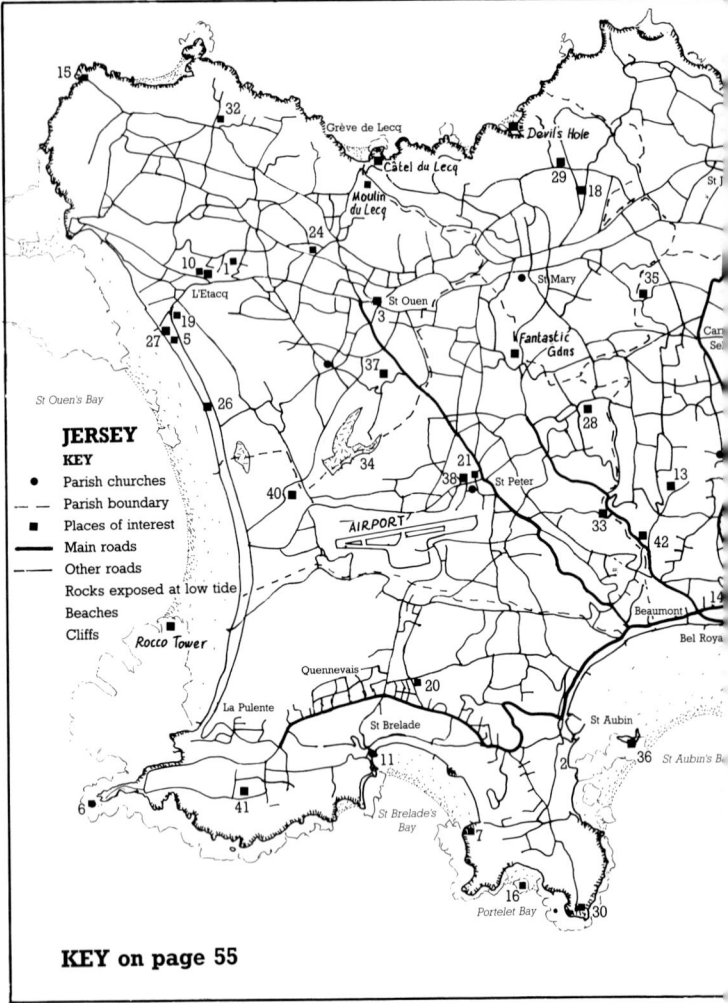

# JERSEY

## KEY

- • Parish churches
- - - Parish boundary
- ■ Places of interest
- ▬ Main roads
- — Other roads
-    Rocks exposed at low tide
-    Beaches
-    Cliffs

## KEY on page 55

St Ouen's Bay

Grève de Lecq
Câtel du Lecq
Moulin du Lecq
Devil's Hole

L'Etacq

St Ouen

St Mary

Fantastic Gdns

St Peter

AIRPORT

Rocco Tower

Quennevais

La Pulente

St Brelade

St Aubin

St Aubin's Bay

Beaumont

Bel Roya

St Brelade's Bay

Portelet Bay

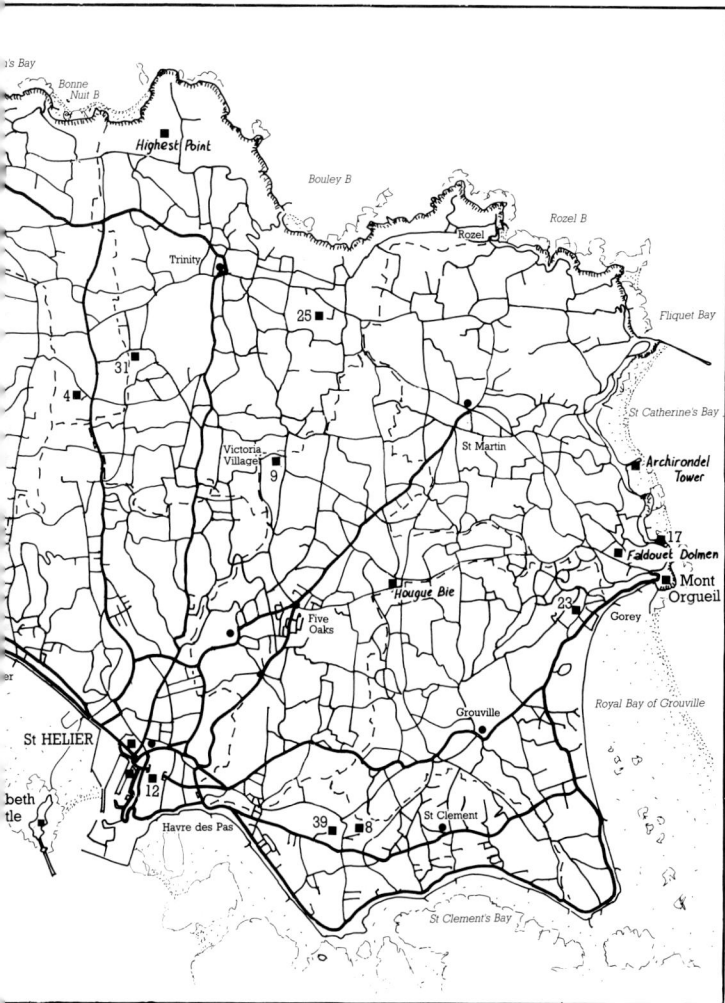

Bonne
Nuit B

Highest Point

Bouley B

Rozel B

Rozel

Trinity

25

Fliquet Bay

31

4

St Catherine's Bay

Victoria
Village

St Martin

Archirondel
Tower

9

17

Faldouet Dolmen

Hougue Bie

Mont
Orgueil

Five
Oaks

23

Gorey

St HELIER

Royal Bay of Grouville

Grouville

beth
tle

12

39    8    St Clement

Havre des Pas

St Clement's Bay

# DISCOVER JERSEY

JERSEY CAN BE SO MANY THINGS to so many people. Archaeologists still find traces of mankind's early occupation here; sportspeople are drawn by a wide range of activities on land, sea, and in the air. Families with young children find the beaches clean and the streets safe; older people delight in seeing the many sights, from prehistoric cairns and medieval castles to the Fort Regent Leisure Centre.

Yet Jersey is still a working island, its industries ranging from the stark extremes of growing new potatoes for the British market, to being one of the leaders of Europe's offshore financial services. This latter business has strict controls designed for customer confidence; for instance, Jersey turned Barlow Clowes away, so it operated its shady deals from Gibraltar. And the Bank of Commerce and Credit International, the infamous BCCI, had two applications refused.

Jersey is wealthy. You won't be here for more than a few hours before you see the evidence in the number of Rolls Royces, despite the narrow roads; the splendid manor houses in the open country, the private aircraft at the airport, the yachts in the marinas, and in St Helier the brass plates of hundreds of international companies registered here. Finance is big business and taxes are low, but don't think of Jersey as a tax haven: the islanders don't like the expression and will tell you so.

**Walks and wildlife.** The States Public Service Committee issues a free leaflet giving broad information on coastal walks, which are: Elizabeth Castle to St Aubin; Noirmont to Belcroute Bay; La Moye Point to Corbière; La Pulente via Grosnez to Rozel; St Catherine's Breakwater to the Archirondel Tower; and Jeffrey's Leap to Grouville golf links. **Guided nature walks** are available at Noirmont, St Catherine's Woods and Les Mielles (Kempt Tower); ask at Kempt Tower May-Sep, Tues-Sun , 1400-1700.

**Island tour.** In our tour of the island, we start in the capital, St Helier, home to one third of the population, and travel clockwise around the parishes: St Lawrence, St Peter, St Brelade in the south-west, St Ouen in the north-west, along the north coast through St Mary, St John and Trinity, then the east coast with St Martin, Grouville, southernmost St Clement and finally St Saviour, the only parish without a coastline.

# 8: St HELIER

### Helibertus's town

MODERN St HELIER is a busy town lying on the coastal plain and dominated by the dome of the Fort Regent Leisure Centre, but the original settlement, and the name, belonged to a 6th-cent monk who settled on Helier's Islet, a tiny outcrop south of the larger **Hermitage Rock,** which now holds Elizabeth Castle.

**Helier, the saint.** History records with some certainty that a certain Helerius or Helibertus was born in Tongeren (Tongres), north-west of Liège, son of a nobleman, but folklore adds that the birth was the result of a miracle performed by the missionary St Cunebert, who then claimed the baby for God. When Cunebert came to collect the young Helerius, the irate father killed the missionary, but the lad left home nonetheless. He wandered to the Cotentin peninsula where he told another missionary, St Marcoulf, of his desire for a life of solitude

## KEY to MAP OF JERSEY on pages 52-53

and penance. Marcoulf recommended Jersey, the island to which he had introduced Christianity in 538.

Helerius settled on his chosen pinnacle, where he supposedly slept in a crevice, St Helier's Bed, near the top, now ringed by the ruins of the 12th cent chapel. Here he became a hermit, fasting much of his time; obviously, as he could forage for food and water only at low tide. The island population was probably no more than 50, due to Saxon, Jute and Viking raiders; St Marcoulf, visiting Helier in 543, allegedly drove off an attack by making the sign of the cross. But in 555 another band of pirates hacked him to death with axes; one legend adds that the hermit picked up his head and walked away, while another claims that his body was washed ashore at Bréville, Normandy, which certainly has a church dedicated to the saint in the French version of his name, Helier.

For centuries, pilgrims kept St Helier's memory alive, and the town that now bears his name remembers its founding saint by the crossed axes in its parish crest, and by a ceremonial pilgrimage to Hermitage Rock on the Sunday closest to 16 July.

# ELIZABETH CASTLE

The great fortress built on Helier's Islet, the small island to the north of Helier's hermitage rock, was begun in earnest in 1594 to supplement Mont Orgueil, which had become vulnerable to land attack from the newer longer-range cannons. The choice of site was fairly obvious, as it was out of range of those menacing cannons, and it would command St Aubin's Bay, the largest sheltered landing beach on the island. It was also where William Fitzhamon, a member of the court of Henry II, had built his Abbey of St Helier around 1155.

**Sir Walter Raleigh.** The castle's new governor, Sir Walter Raleigh, named the defence Fort Isabella Bellissima, the 'most beautiful Elizabeth,' in honour of his queen.

Paul Ivy, who had already fortified Kinsale in Ireland and Cornwall's Falmouth, was in charge of the construction. By 1601 he had presented Raleigh with a complete castle, now known as the **Upper Ward** and occupying the highest part of Helier's Islet at its southern tip.

Ivy continued working, and within two years he had added the curtain walls enclosing an area down to Elizabeth Gate, and a platform, now called **Raleigh's Yard,** which had a field of fire covering the site of the future harbour. Then came the large Governor's House which Raleigh made his official residence until he was recalled by the new monarch, James I, ultimately to spend another 15 years in the Tower of London.

Successor Governor Sir Philippe de Carteret, who held the

*Queen Elizabeth's Gate at Elizabeth Castle leads to Hermitage Rock and the breatwater.*

defences between 1626 and 1636, added the **Lower Ward,** whose curtain walls enclosed the middle of the island, with the Governor's House and Fitzhamon's abbey of 1155. Access to this ward was originally over a drawbridge.

Further work around 1646 added **Fort Charles** at the northernmost tip, named from the future Charles II who paid his first visit to Jersey that year: the fort is beside the modern entrance at **Landward Gate.** In 1668 the curtain walls were extended again to give more cannon emplacements, this new work becoming the **Outer Ward,** which protected the remaining northern part of Helier's Islet and sealed in the Green with its fortified windmill.

**First action.** Elizabeth Castle first saw action not against the obvious enemy in France, but during the Civil War in England when Sir George Carteret held it as one of the last two Royalist strongholds in the English realm, Guernsey's Castle Cornet being the other. Then on 21 October 1651 Cromwell's Parliamentarians under Admiral Robert Blake landed in St Ouen's Bay and soon began the bombardment of Elizabeth Castle with mortars. The fortress had been built to place it beyond the reach of land-based artillery, yet on 9 November one mortar bomb went through the roof of the **Abbey of St Helier** in the Lower Ward, penetrated to the crypt where it exploded, destroying not only vital ammunition and food, but Fitzhamon's abbey itself, the site now being marked by a cross on the barrack square. Five weeks later, Sir George was forced to surrender, but the

Royalists in Guernsey's Castle Cornet held out for four more days, so becoming the last outpost to surrender to Cromwell.

Further defensive posts were added in the 18th cent, particularly the barrack block and several gates and moats, giving us the castle as seen today, except for the remaining German additions.

## ELIZABETH CASTLE TODAY

The castle, known in some circles as one of Western Europe's finest fortifications, is approachable at all states of the tide. At low water a hard causeway 1,100m long, gives around five hours' sightseeing, but when the sea begins to encroach an amphibious vehicle takes over, reducing travelling time to a few minutes.

The castle is **open** Easter-Oct 0930-1800, the rather large fee covering admission to all parts. Visitors enter through the **Landward Gate,** above which is the Castle Bell, formerly rung half an hour before the tide began to cover the causeway. King William's Gate opens onto the Green, a large space giving access to a wide range of artillery including French 110mm guns captured at the Maginot Line in World War One, carronades (cannons) that fired 32lb (14.5kg) balls, and a 6.5ton muzzle-loaded cannon with a 7in (178mm) bore, brought here to defend Jersey against Napoleon. The Germans added their own weaponry, but that has gone.

The Lower Ward holds the **Royal Jersey Militia Regimental Museum** in the former Gymnasium, while the old Barrack has the **Granite and Gunpowder** exhibition holding yet more weapons from medieval to modern, including some left by the Germans. The Governor's House has a tableau showing the castle's history, mainly in the form of wax dummies including one of Raleigh himself, discussing the building plans with Paul Ivy.

The Iron Gate leads to Raleigh's Yard, from where you can walk to the **Upper Keep** and the German control tower, preserved because it is as much a part of history as the oldest stone in Ivy's structure. Finally, Elizabeth's Gate opens out to the breakwater and Helier's Hermitage Rock, where the hermit's cleft, near the top of the 89ft (27m) pinnacle, is still enclosed in the ruins of a 12th-cent chapel.

A bizarre touch of modern history is enshrined in the castle in a notice painted in English:

> Any persons found marking walls with V-signs or insults against the German Armed Forces are liable to be shot.
> G.V.Schmettow, General,
> German Military Government.

# THE TOWN

The town of St Helier didn't need the protection of Elizabeth Castle as it was very small; even 140 years after Paul Ivy began building, it had less than 600 houses. The harbour was equally unimportant; before 1700, when what is now the Old South Pier was begun, creating the English and French harbours, ships beached at **Havre des Pas.** George II gave £200 in 1751 to help finance port expansion, for which act he is remembered in Royal Square, yet the Old North Pier was not added until 1790. Between 1841 and '53 the Victoria and Albert piers extended the docking area, with the Castle Breakwater coming in 1887 to protect the harbour from prevailing south-westerly gales.

**Liberation Square.** The focal point of modern St Helier is undoubtedly Liberation Square, until recently known as The Weigh-bridge although the weighing device has long since gone, leaving a small car park in the midst of some of the busiest traffic on the island.

## RAILWAYS

The smart building on the north-west side of Liberation Square holds the **Tourist Office** but it was originally the station for the **Jersey Railway Company** which in 1870 started laying a track from here along the coast to St Aubin, perhaps the easiest place in all the Channel Islands to put a railway line. In 1884 the owners did the seemingly impossible by pushing the line over the 200ft contour on its way west, ending first at La Moye and, with a last thrust, reaching La Corbière in 1899; much of the course of this section of line survives as a pleasant walking route. But even before this final stretch was laid, the several changes in ownership indicated that this was not a highly profitable venture; at one time the line's proprietor was the man who also ran the Guernsey Railway Company, which was doing no better.

The last train from St Helier into St Aubin in the 1936 season arrived on 30 September. It was also the last train the JRC was ever to run as, 18 days later, St Aubin station and much of the rolling stock were destroyed by fire.

Meanwhile, the **Jersey Eastern Railway** started in 1873 from Snow Hill at the northern tip of Mount Bingham (Fort Regent), laying tracks around the southern coast towards Gorey which it reached 18 years later. Lacking other scope for expansion, the company then operated the boat to France which connected with the train to Paris. But in 1929 the railway part of the venture closed, with the shipping line soon to follow. Probably the most interesting anecdote is that the line's one-time manager was a Major Gilbert More, father of the actor Kenneth More.

**German resurrection.** The occupying Wehrmacht needed rail-ways to transport the vast amount of granite, cement and weaponry it consumed in defending Jersey against an attack which didn't come, so

**St HELIER**

N

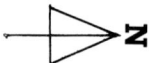

No entry for cars
Pedestrianised

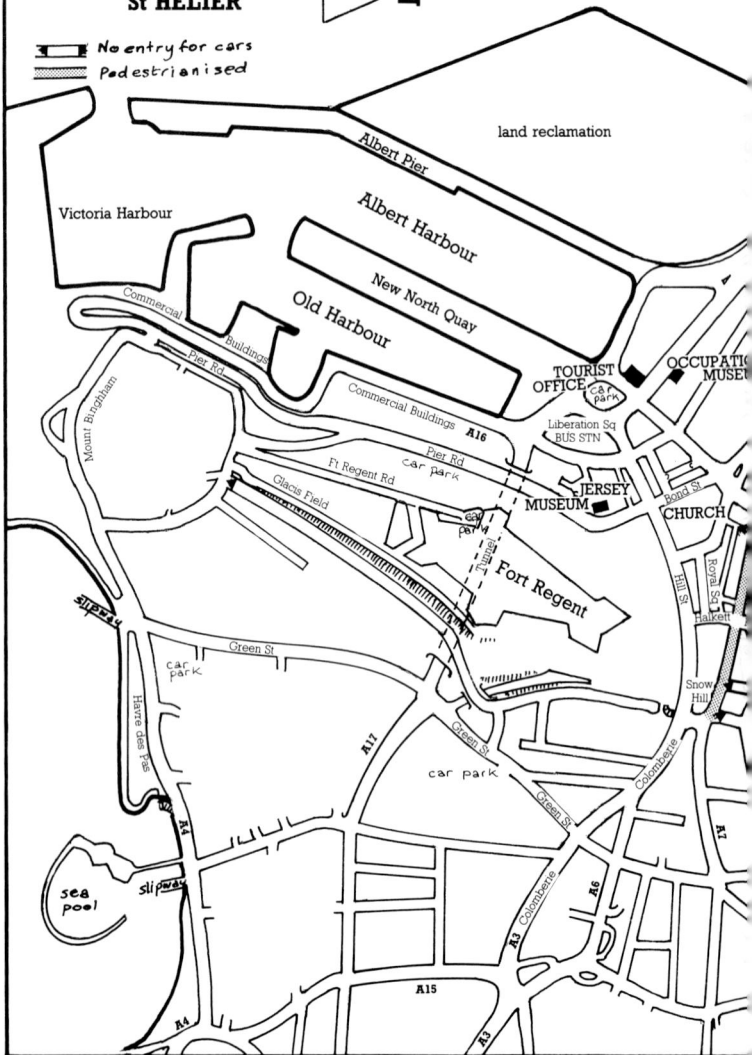

land reclamation

Albert Pier

Albert Harbour

Victoria Harbour

New North Quay

Commercial

Old Harbour

Buildings

Pier Rd

Commercial Buildings A16

TOURIST OFFICE
car park

OCCUPATION MUSEUM

Liberation Sq
BUS STN

Mount Bingham

Pier Rd
car park

Ft Regent Rd

Glacis Field

car park

JERSEY MUSEUM

Bond St

CHURCH

Fort Regent

Tunnel

Hill St

Royal Sq

Halkett

slipway

Green St

car park

Snow Hill

Harre des Pas

A17

Green St

Colomberie

car park

Green St

A4

sea pool

slipway

Colomberie

A3

A6

A7

A15

A3

A4

*You cannot learn French by studying these bilingual street names. New Cut's earlier name could be translated as 'Dunce's Corner.'*

it rebuilt the railways, using metre-gauge for the JRC line from St Helier to Corbière which was reopened in July 1942, and for an extension far grander than the original builders would have dreamed of; northwards, passing St Peter's Bunker to St Mary, and on to Ronez Quarry on the north coast, the source of much of their building stone. From near the Fantastic Gardens they built a spur line down to St Ouen's Bay, passing Sunset Nurseries. From here a 60cm-gauge line ran south to La Pulente at the foot of the Corbière hills, conveniently passing the quarry at La Carrière, whose name is French for 'quarry,' while the same 60cm line also ran north to further quarries near the craft shops at L'Etacq.

The Germans reopened the JER to Gorey and laid a short spur to a source of stone near Les Maltières. In the few years of their operation under German control these lines carried far more freight than when they were run as commercial ventures – but the Germans were not concerned with profit and loss. During the war they moved 255,000 cubic metres of material to build the Atlantic Wall on the European mainland, while they quarried 244,000 cubic metres in the Channel Islands – including Guernsey and Alderney – a figure which fell some way below the target.

To do this, they were obliged to rebuild the railways in Guernsey, in one instance running through a glasshouse which was allowed to remain, and on Alderney, which is now the only surviving railway in the islands, re-rebuilt to standard gauge and using London Underground rolling stock for carriages.

# FORT REGENT

Drive east from Liberation Square and within a minute you're in the tunnel carved under Mount Bingham, upon which sits Fort Regent. To visit this bastion built to keep Napoleon at bay, you need to drive south and come up Fort Regent Road to the car park, unless it's already full. On foot, your best approach is from Snow Hill in the north, where elevators offer an alternative to the steep ramp, as the cable car is not operating.

Today this old bastion is the **Fort Regent Leisure Centre,**, capped by a dome 190ft (58m) in diameter. There was considerable local opposition to the conversion, some people referring to it as the Jersey white elephant, but at a cost of around £4,000,000 the project went ahead, giving the island its largest concentration of family entertainment. Throughout the summer season there are live daytime activities, except on Monday; evening entertainment targeted at the entire family; top-name performers in the 2,000-seat Gloucester Hall which can double as a sports arena; and a wide range of other attractions, which make the centre a miniature version of an American theme park.

The schedule is subject to change, but you should have a selection which includes The Lillie Langtry Story, The German Bunker, the World of the Sea with its own sharks, Humfrey's Playland which recalls the fort's architect John Hambly Humfrey, a fairground, and much more. The season is Easter to early October.

# ROYAL SQUARE

If Liberation Square is the focal point of St Helier, Royal Square is certainly its centre, as the gilt statue of George II standing here is the spot from which all distances are measured and the reason for the square having its regal name. King George, dressed as a Roman emperor yet wearing the Order of the Garter, is honoured for his gift of £200 to improve the harbour, but when his statue was unveiled here in July 1751, Royal Square was still called Le Marché, 'The Market,' and was frequently criticised for its filth, dropped by horses, poultry and other livestock, with the addition of rubbish scattered by humans.

Market places have been the setting for many activities other than selling merchandise, and condemned witches were executed here in the mid-17th cent. Later in the century, prisoners were clamped in the stocks here for the public to hurl filth and abuse at them.

**Peirson.** It was in January 1781 that Major Francis Peirson and Baron de Rullecourt died here in the Battle of Jersey. Peirson had first seized Mount Bingham – the fort had yet to be built – then led his troops along Broad St to Rue de Derrière (now King St), and through a gap known as Peirson Place, to the Market. The nearby public house, now the *Peirson,* probably received more bullets than any other building during the brief battle.

*Bride and groom would carve their initials and the year of their marriage in lintel-stones in their new home. NN wed EST in 1840.*

**New Market.** The States bought a site on Halkett Place in 1796, and by 1800 the market had moved, leaving Le Marché to become Royal Square.

**Royal Court.** The States followed this clearance by rebuilding its offices along the southern side of the square – which is decidedly longer than square – including the ornate Royal Court, completed in 1866. The courthouse is on record as having been on this site in 1309 when St Helier town was little more than a collection of primitive huts, and the present building is open to visitors during normal sessions, with the public entrance on Halkett Place beneath the arms of George II. During court proceedings, look for the bailiff's mace, a gift from Charles II, and elsewhere a copy of John Copley's famous painting, *The Death of Major Peirson*. A legend claims that the babe in arms on the right of the picture was to be the great-grandmother of Lillie Langtry.

Twice a year the Royal Court is the scene of a private ceremony when at the *Assise d'Héritage* the seigneurs of the island fiefs renew their oaths of loyalty to the crown, another relic of feudal times that survives into the modern age.

**Public Library.** The library, founded in 1736, is at the western end of Royal Place in a building dating from 1886. The benefactor, the Rev Philip Falle, included a number of 16th-cent books in his bequest.

*Elizabeth Castle's Outer Ward (above) seen from the Keep, with St Helier in the distance, contrasting with St Helier's pedestrianised shopping precinct at the height of summer.*

St Aubin's Harbour at low tide (above) is picturesque, but of no commercial use. The Corbière lighthouse (below) is on an island at high tide.

## THE PARISH CHURCH

St Helier's parish church is, of course, dedicated to the hermit Helerius, whose statue stands over the north door. The warm red granite church, the *Chapelle de Saint Hélier,* stands very close to Royal Square, and the remains of Major Peirson are buried in its tiny cemetery. The original church has records of receiving tithes for William, Duke of Normandy, before he conquered England in 1066; the present church is mainly 14th cent but incorporating parts of the 11th-cent chantry and 12th-cent chapels. It was consecrated in 1341 and restored heavily between 1846 and '68, and it is claimed that some of the churchyard railings were formerly a screen separating male and female prisoners in the old Newgate St Prison chapel.

**Sanctuary.** The ancient right of *perquage* applied to St Helier's church as to all the other 11 parish churches on the island, but there was no need of protected escape routes from St Brelade and St Helier, as both churches were built on the shoreline.

## JERSEY MUSEUM

A little way south of the church, off Caledonia Place, the Jersey Museum occupies an impressive building completed in 1992 and linking the Merchant's House at 9 Pier Road with the 18th-cent warehouse, *La Longue Caserne,* both of which are to be restored. The museum is also the headquarters of the *Société Jersiaise,* founded in 1873.

**Lillie Langtry.** A ground-floor room is devoted to mementos of Emily Charlotte le Breton, who became famous as Lillie Langtry. Emily was born to Dean le Breton, rector of St Saviour church, in 1853. She was the girl whose delicate complexion, then in high fashion, caused her to be known by her familiarised first name, Lillie – *not* Lily – while still at school. Shortly after she married Edward Langtry at St Saviour's Church at the age of 21, she and her husband went to London and joined the social set. It was here that she met the Jersey artist Sir John Millais who painted her holding a lily and so created her popular name, the 'Jersey Lily.'

**Royal lovers.** She soon became notorious for her lovers, who included the Prince of Wales, later to be King Edward VII (1901-'10), Oscar Wilde – but *he* was a homosexual – and Louis Mountbatten, who fathered a child by her. This Mountbatten also fathered Lord Louis, the last Viceroy of India, giving Lillie another tenuous link with royalty. The museum has as an exhibit the pithy comment from a lord of the realm, commenting on the loss of Lillie's parrot: "I didn't know she'd had a parrot, though I'd heard she'd had a cockatoo." *Cockatoo* was the current slang for 'cuckold' or lover.

Lillie spent too much of her husband's money and was soon forced to earn a living. She chose the theatre, making her debut at

Twickenham Town Hall where, although she muffed her lines, she was applauded for her porcelain beauty. Lillie Langtry the actress was to be adulated from London to the Antipodes.

She played in South Africa, bought a ranch in California, toured the USA so often that she had her own railroad carriage, the *Lalee*, and gave her name to a Texan village which has since changed it. She owned a steam yacht and was the first female member of the Royal Channel Islands Yacht Club. She bought a cottage in St Aubin and named it *Merman* from her horse which won the 1897 Cesarewitch and £39,000.

Marrying for the second time in her parish church of St Saviour, she became Lady de Bathe, then retired to a life of leisure in Monaco, where she died in 1929. Her body was brought back to St Saviour and lies in the churchyard under a lily-white marble bust.

**Victor Hugo.** Born in Besançon in 1802 of a Royalist mother and a major in Bonaparte's Republican army, it was no surprise that Victor Hugo had divided loyalties. He received the *Légion d'Honneur* in 1837, was elected to the *Académie Française* and, after Louis-Philippe was dethroned, he found himself in the *Assemblée Nationale*, the republican government. Eventually his liberalism dominated his thinking, forcing him into exile in Brussels then, in 1852, to a house at Havre des Pas, Jersey, with his mistress Juliette Drouet discreetly nearby. He and his fellow exiles met by a large boulder to plot against Napoleon III; the boulder is now marked with a plaque and known as *Le Rocher des Proscrits*, 'Outlaws' Rock.'

*Elizabeth Castle silhouetted against the southern horizon.*

*St Aubin's Fort is not open to the public, but you can wander around the outside at low tide.*

The museum traces some of the tumultuous years of this man who wrote *Les Misérables* and, in its English translation, *The Hunchback of Notre Dame,* as well as many other works. In Jersey he voiced his support for the local publication *L'Homme,* the organ of radical French exiles, and after Queen Victoria visited the island he wrote to her, courtesy of *L'Homme:*

> For the price of the respect in which we hold the law of your country, permit us to offer you some useful reflections on your visit. But first, a word of congratulation. By the grace of God you have returned safe and sound, and you should realise this was not without some risk to you.

Hugo was expelled soon after, in October 1955, and moved to Guernsey where he lived for 14 years before returning to France.

**Other exhibits.** The museum concentrates on the island's history, culture and wildlife, but also has the Barreau Art Gallery, the Ship Room, and the T.B.Davis Room which tells the story of the racing schooner *Westwood,* a prizewinner in the decade from 1925 but which was scuttled off Alderney in 1947 for lack of a buyer. Other exhibits of note are in the Marine Biology Room and its adjacent chamber of horrors which has a 12-man wooden treadmill taken from the now-demolished Newgate Street Prison in town.

The museum is open Mon-Sat 1000-1800, Sun 1400-1800, ~1700 in winter.

## SEEING St HELIER

Queen St and King St and parts of nearby streets which form the main shopping centre of the town, are pedestrianised. Small flower gardens, old-style signposts and waste bins add to the charm, but parking your car is a major problem.

**Markets.** Undoubtedly the best way to see the town centre is on foot, and it is certainly the only way to see the covered Central Market on Halkett Place, built to take the traders from what is now Royal Square. The present market building, with decorative cast iron pillars supporting a glass roof, was built in 1882 to mark the centenary of the Battle of Jersey, and looks typically Victorian. Beresford Market, on the north side of Beresford St, was opened in 1841 as a fish market, and is probably still the best place to buy your seafood.

**Occupation Museum.** St Helier's Occupation Museum is at 9, The Esplanade; there are other mementos of those grim war years at St Peter's Bunker, the Underground Hospital, Lewis Tower and Kempt Tower on St Ouen's Bay, the Strawberry Farm, Elizabeth Castle and the Hougue Bie, but don't let that deter you from seeing the one in town. Here the theme appeals directly to the visitor from Britain with the question: what might have happened had Hitler invaded the mainland? "It was a near thing!" the museum adds. In addition to the expected displays of small arms, there are remnants of equipment buried for years in tunnels at St Peter, and reminders of how the islanders lived, not knowing at the outset whether liberation would come in their lifetime. Original letters and documents add colour to this grim story, but the main exhibit is a video, compiled by Channel Television, of people reliving their experiences under the Nazi jackboot.

## OUT OF TOWN

St Helier parish has few places of interest outside the town but, travelling north-west along the coast on the inland A1, you may stop to see megalithic monuments in St Andrew's churchyard at First Tower near the start of the road called Mont Cochon – 'Mount Pig.' The Ville-ès-Nouaux burial sites yielded Bronze Age beakers and cremation urns in the 1869 excavation.

# 9: SOUTH and WEST

## Sts Lawrence, Peter and Brelade

THIS PART OF JERSEY has the best beaches and some splendid cliff scenery, as well as the islets holding St Aubin's Fort, Janvrin's Tomb, and the Corbière lighthouse.

### St LAWRENCE

**Glass Church.** Coming from St Helier you are scarcely in the parish when you reach the Glass Church, the unusual memorial to Jesse Boot, the founder of the Boots chain store. Jesse was born in Nottingham in 1850, and opened his first pharmacy when he was 27. His idea was well-timed and his business sense so acute that soon every major town in Britain had its branch of Boots the Chemists. Boot, later to become the first Baron Trent, married Florence, a Jersey girl, and it was she who decided that her husband's memorial was to be the complete renovation of a church interior, using glass.

The original St Matthew's Church was built in 1840 to avoid the need for people living on the coast to walk inland to the parish church, but in 1934 Lady Trent renovated it using the moulded and frosted, but not opaque, glass of René Lalique, a Parisian whose style was then popular. The Glass Church has a 12ft (4m) glass cross above a glass altar, supported by glass pillars. The font, the pillars beside the doorway, much of the door itself, and a large window, are all cast in Lalique's unique glass, which hints at the Jersey lily – the plant, not the actress – in some of its mouldings.

This was Lalique's only major venture into church archiecture, and the results are open daily except during services, with a small car park nearby.

Lady Trent also created the nearby **Coronation Park,** giving it to the island in 1937 as a permanent haven for the young and the old.

**Bel Royal.** Bel Royal house, on the north side of St Aubin's Rd, the A1, has a sundial dated 1794, but your main association with Bel Royal will be the strange crossroads forcing incoming westbound A2 traffic onto the outgoing westbound A1, and incoming westbound A1 traffic onto the outgoing northbound A11. Incoming eastbound A1 traffic can go north on A11 or continue eastbound on A2 – see the map to sort out the complications.

**Watermills.** So, coming westbound from the Glass Church you are forced inland on the A11, to the **Tesson Mill,** a five-storey building which has been restored but is not open to the public. This mill, like the others on the island, most of which are in St Lawrence, originally belonged to the monarch but was handed out as a *fief du roy* to a seigneur or an abbey. Tenants of the fief were obliged to grind their wheat at the local mill, and supply materials and labour for its maintenance.

**Quetivel Mill.** The A11 continues up St Peter's Valley and, on the parish boundary, passes Quetivel Mill, not only restored by the Jersey National Trust, but open Apr-Oct Tues-Thur 1000–1600. The first watermill on this site was known to be working in 1309, and there are records of a baker known as Guillaume de Keytovel in 1307; the present mill operated until the mid-19th cent but its machinery was in decay until the Germans restored it and brought Quetivel back into use to supplement the flour rations coming from France. Fire ravaged it after the war, leading to the latest restoration as Jersey's only working watermill. Don't confuse it with another Quetivel Mill in the north of the parish.

## UNDERGROUND HOSPITAL

Turn right at Tesson Mill onto the B89 and you are on the road to probably the largest tourist attraction in the island, the German Underground Military Hospital. Half a century after it was built it is still stark and forbidding, thereby adding to its popularity with visitors.

This was the grimmest side of the German Occupation, a gaunt hospital carved out of the solid rock by hundreds of civilian slave labourers, including prisoners from the Spanish Civil War, occupied Europe west and east, and allegedly women and children from Ukraine and Russia. These most miserable of human wretches, out of reach of the Geneva Convention, were stabled on the same marshland at Goose Green where Lord Hambye had slain his legendary dragon, and were forced to hack out 14,000 tons (272,000 cu ft, 7,000 cu m) of rock to make the world's most impregnable hospital. The work took 2½ years, yet none of the labourers was eligible to receive any benefit from the hospital: fed less than subsistence diet on six days, and going hungry on their day of rest, hundreds of these humans without hope died where they worked and were buried in concrete where they fell.

The hospital was to have four parallel tunnels each 100m long, linked at right-angles by seven smaller tunnels. Two of the main shafts were completed, giving access to an operating theatre, several wards, and other rooms, but the unfinished shafts are preserved as they were found in 1945, rough-hewn, with rotting roof supports

*Tesson Mill, St Lawrence, restored by the Jersey National Trust.*

(there's no danger of roof collapse) and now with a background accompaniment of the moaning of the damned adding a tingle of apprehension to the atmosphere.

A sign evokes more sympathy: *Under these conditions men of many nations laboured to construct this hospital. Those who survived will never forget; those who did not will never be forgotten.*

**Barracks.** Ironically, the tunnels were planned as barracks for artillerymen, and German soldiers began the drilling in 1941. The Organization Todt was called in when work was seen to be going too slowly, and the first slave labourers from occupied Europe arrived soon after. It was in early 1944 that the labyrinth was converted to a hospital, for which it was never used, as the place was abandoned shortly before the Allied invasion of Normandy in June 1944: it is doubtful if patients would have recovered properly out of reach of sunlight despite the central heating system.

Within the hospital a small museum shows other aspects of life under occupation, telling in particular the story of how British-born Channel Islanders suffered in concentration camps in Germany after their deportation, while another exhibit concentrates on the bizarre life that childen led during those lean years.

71

There is a large car park with toilets, and the hospital is open daily 0930-1730, less in winter.

## WATERWORKS VALLEY and the CENTRE STONE

Three roads lead inland from the southern coast, where most of St Lawrence's people live. They are the A11, which goes on to St Mary, the A10 to St John, and the C118, on the boundary with St Helier, which offers a pleasant drive up the steep-sided and wooded **Waterworks Valley,** holding the Millbrook Reservoir built in 1898, the Dannemarche of 1909 and the Handois Reservoir finished in 1932. This is one of the quietest parts of the island although the centre of bustling St Helier is less than two miles away.

Beyond Dannemarche, quiet lanes lead east to the **Centre Stone,** although access is better along the A9 from St Helier. Coming from the south on the A9, look for the gaunt Sion (sic) Methodist Chapel on the left, built in 1880, and take the next left; coming from the north, look for St John's Congregational Church on the left, then take the next right. Along Rue des Servais watch for the **Centre House** on the left and continue another 65m. The small stone which marks the central point of the island is at the base of a wall in La Chasse Cottage, and is believed to have been brought from a hougue long since destroyed.

Nearby attraction: Pallot's Steam Museum in Trinity.

## St LAWRENCE CHURCH

The A10 leads to the parish church, on the site of a Norman chapel. The parish to the north is St John, but it was *this* church that John, younger brother of Richard I, and Lord of the Isles in his own right, gave to the Abbey Blanchelande in Normandy in 1198, which held it until the Reformation. The church grew slowly over the ages, the nave being added in the 14th cent, the chapel in 1524 as shown by the date carved in the north-east buttress, and the chancel built in the 15th cent. The bell, cast in 1592, is the oldest in Jersey.

## RETREAT FARM CARNATIONS

Retreat Farm Carnations, also trading as the Jersey Flower Centre in the north-west corner of the parish, claims to be the largest grower of carnations in the British Isles and the largest mail-order florist in the world. Its biggest glasshouse, open to visitors' inspection, covers 5 acres (20,500sq m) and holds almost 300,000 plants – and there are two smaller glasshouses.

Come here for flower-arranging demonstrations, to learn how to create a semi-arid garden, or to check up on many aspects of wildlife in the flamingo lake, the wildfowl sanctuary, or the koi carp reserve. Open daily Apr-Oct 0930-1730; ample free parking.

Nearby attractions: Living Legend and Fantastic Gardens in St Peter, Jersey Butterflies in St Mary.

# St PETER

The first aircraft to land in Jersey used the beach of St Aubin's Bay as a runway. The event was part of an aerial race from St Malo on 26 August 1912, won by Jean Benoît. As a contrast, the modern airport in St Peter's parish is large enough to handle short-haul jet aircraft.

## St PETER'S BUNKER and JERSEY MOTOR MUSEUM

Two tourist attractions stand almost wall-to-wall in the centre of the village, a little to the north of the runway. St Peter's Bunker changed its name from the Occupation Museum to avoid confusion with other such locations, and the Jersey Motor Museum is also known as the Car Museum.

The **bunker,** built in 1942 to command this major crossroads and guard the airport approach, housed 33 men in seven small rooms, all of which now hold what is claimed to be the largest collection of Occupation relics in Jersey. The part-underground bunker has been used in location shots for numerous films, and its Enigma decoding machine, one of the few surviving, has featured in other films.

As a museum of the Occupation, it gives graphic details of island life between 1 July 1940 and 10 May 1945, including many manufactured necessities of life that the people had to replace for themselves, from shoes and radios to saucepans.

The **Motor Museum** displays cars – Jaguars, Rolls-Royces, an early Talbot, and many more – but that's only a part of it. Many of the vehicles have historical connections, such as the Phantom III that General Bernard Montgomery used while planning the Normandy landings, and cars that the Germans abandoned at the war's end. There's also a carriage saved from the Jersey Railway Company.

Both displays are open Mar-Sep daily 1000-1700 and share a car park.

### St PETER'S CHURCH

The tallest spire in the Channel Islands – 122ft, 37m – is so close to the flight path of the islands' busiest airport that St Peter's must carry a red warning light. Beginning life as San Pietro in Deserto because of the dunes to the west, the original chapel on this site was raised to the status of a church on the orders of Duke William of Normandy shortly before he conquered England. But the duke also ordered that half the tithes be paid to the convent in Caen.

Some of the stones of that chapel's walls are still visible in the chancel, but the remainder of the building has been added over the centuries: the nave and transepts in the 12th cent, giving the building its cross-shape. The chapel is 14th cent, the south aisle from the 15th cent, and the north aisle 19th cent. The bell, cast in Normandy in 1649, carries the inscription *Mon nom est Elizabeth la belle,* probably referring to Lady Elizabeth Carteret, who was closely involved in parish affairs as well as being the wife of the governor who defended a castle named Elizabeth. The French for 'bell' is *cloche,* so it's doubtful if a pun was intended.

## LIVING LEGEND

Half a cross-country mile east of the village centre, at La Rue du Petit Aleval, the Living Legend opened in 1992 with the claim to be Jersey's most exciting visitor attraction. To whet the appetite further, this £8,000,000 investment has a sign warning: *if you are faint-hearted or of a nervous disposition, do not venture beyond* the entrance.

As you are bound to be more intrigued than nervous, you find yourself taking an active part in tracing the island's history, as well as some of its legends, by walking the deck of a Victorian paddle steamer, seeing Lord Hambye slay his dragon, reliving the Battle of Jersey...there's so *much* to do, and quite a range of buildings in which to do it, all of them opening from a large T-shaped courtyard.

The Norman Conquest, Charles II's exile on the island, the German Occupation, Lillie Langtry, and smuggling and privateering are among the subjects brought to life, your experience among the living legend culminating in a 20-minute show. The financing company, Diamond Jersey, called in the creators of the Jorvik Centre in York, the Last Labyrinth at Land's End, and designers of sets for the Bond

*Kempt Tower on St Ouen's Bay is a miniature museum.*

films to create the desired effect, and has also built a typical Jersey manor house on this 9-acre (4ha) site in the open countryside.

Open daily 0930-1530, with provisions for children and ♿ visitors. Fee around £3.50.

## FANTASTIC TROPICAL GARDENS

The Fantastic Gardens snuggle into a shallow depression in the vingtaine of Augurez, at the head of St Peter's Valley, and you get your passport at the entrance. Passport? Certainly, for the gardens are divided into six countries, beginning with Spain and going on to include Japan, China, Morocco, India, Thailand, Mexico and Zaire – that's more than six, but the destinations change. The theme is horticulture, but the plot really is sheer fantasy, with side excursions to see Thai dancers, the Parrot Show featuring Birdjerac and Lillie Langtry, the singing caballero in Mexico, the *African Queen* that's nearly as good as the original in the Florida Keys, a seven-foot Buddha, and the Stanley Falls in Zaire. And then there's the Boot Hill Ghoulf Club.

For something that's certainly different, come and sample a taste of fantasy, daily Apr-Oct from 0900 until the fun ceases some time in the evening. Ample parking.

## SUNSET NURSERIES

Sunset Nurseries is aptly named as it faces the setting sun across the middle of St Ouen's Bay, and on clear evenings you can see the earth's shadow climb the hills behind. As evidence of the exposed site, the business had 18 tons of glass broken by the hurricane which struck south-east England on 16 October 1987.

This is a commercial nursery growing carnations in eight glasshouses and alstromeria in another, with the added attraction of a tropical aviary, trout pools, and a restaurant serving srawberries and cream for as long a season as possible. Open daily 1000-1700 except winter weekends, so you must see the sun go down from outside the gate.

## St OUEN'S BAY DEFENCES

The British and German defences along the four-mile (6.5km) stretch of St Ouen's Bay oddly called Five Mile Road, extend into the parishes of St Brelade, St Peter and St Ouen itself. The British built most of the towers in the early 19th cent, anticipating an invasion by the French, with Tower No 2 being the work of Sir James Kempt, master-general of ordnance, from whom it was named in 1834. The **Kempt Tower** is open May-Sep Tues-Sun 1400-1700, and Apr & Oct Thur and Sun only, free, mounting a static exhibition showing how the occupying Germans adapted these forts for mid-20th-cent warfare. The Wehrmacht added a string of other defences at the foot of the hills to the east: Morville Haus, Thiebault, Hühnengrab ('Chicken's Grave'), Ville au Bas, Doktor Haus, one at the disused La Mare Mill by Sunset Nurseries, St Peters Baracken, Düne, and two called Höhe ('High') on the golf links of St Brelade. And in 1943 they started using La Rocco Tower for target practise. La Rocco was built in 1800, 800m out to sea.

The Germans built a bunker by Tower No 1, Lewis Tower, which is now a Military Museum.

# St BRELADE

St Brelade is arguably the most interesting of Jersey's parishes. It commands splendid views across St Aubin's Bay from above the village, and of St Brelade's Bay from the headlands at each end. The cliffs around Noirmont and Corbière are rugged and scenic, and the vingtaine of **Les Quennevais** is Jersey's second most important shopping area yet without the congestion associated with St Helier.

**Hemp.** This district takes its name from the Jersiaise word for 'hemp,' *chènevière*, which was grown here until the St Catherine's Day (25 November) storm of 1492 covered the area with sand from St Ouen's Bay and its hinterland. In 1668 another sandstorm forced farmers to abandon their land, which was unusable until marram grasses were planted around 1800 to bind the shifting sands. It may be more than coincidence that the French for 'hemp' is *chanvre*, so similar to the name Janvrin, forever associated with the nearby Ile au Guerdain.

**Menhirs.** Several Neolithic standing stones survive in the area, notably those north and west of Les Quennevais which may be boundary markers, way markers or headstones of graves. Others have been lost to builders over the centuries.

**La Cotte de St Brelade.** Above Ouaisné Bay, the eastern part of St Brelade's Bay, a sea cave 60ft (18m) above the present tides, has been dated to 150,000 years old, carved during the last but one Ice Age. Flint tools and animal bones infer that Palaeolithic Man lived here during a warm period several millennia later, hunting mammoth which came over on the land link from France. The finds are in the Jersey Museum, and although the cave, discovered in 1881, is closed to casual visitors the area itself is popular, offering a car park by the Smugglers Inn, and a good beach with deck chair hire.

# St AUBIN

St Aubin is a beautiful village built around the junction of Route de la Haule, the A1 coast road; Mont les Vaux, 'Valley Hill,' the A13; and Le Boulevard, which fronts onto the picturesque harbour. The roads meet at Charing Cross, near where the railway station stood and from where the northern breakwater forms part of the harbour protection.

The village shares its patron saint, a 6th-cent Bishop of Angers, with the town of Aubin near Rodez in the French *département* of Aveyron and miles from the sea. This is odd, as Aubin the saint is the guardian of people seeking protection from pirates attacking from the sea; it is also ironic as in the 17th cent St Aubin's harbour was often crowded with privateers (legalised pirate ships) and their spoils, mainly French. Sir George Carteret was prominent among the entrepreneurs as this was how he paid for the maintenance of Mont Orgueil and Elizabeth Castle.

St Aubin outclassed St Helier in importance in the 17th and 18th cents because of its port, the southern arm being built around 1675 (the present pier dates from 1754) and the northern in 1819.

The harbour is flooded only at the top of the tide, which makes it commercially unviable but attractive for yachtsmen without deep-keel vessels. The village featured prominently in the TV series *Bergerac*, with The Old Coach House Restaurant on the waterfront becoming famous as 'Diamond Lil's' in early programmes. The Channel Islands did not need the stage coach system which developed in England and France; indeed, there was no road between here and St Helier until General Don opened his military road in 1844.

**Rozel. If you're lucky you can park by the water's edge.**

There is history at every turn. The narrow High St, tucked away north of Charing Cross, has some of the oldest houses in the village, the Terminus Hotel and rail station is now the colourful parish hall on the north pier, and the covered market, built in 1826, now holds the NatWest Bank; look for the alms-slot by the door, with its plaque *Souvenez-vous des Pauvres,* 'remember the poor.' At Quai Bisson, off the Boulevard, St Aubin's Woollen Mill claims to be the only manufacturer of jerseys in Jersey.

**St Aubin's Fort.** The first defences on the little island 500m offshore and on the edge of the low-tide zone, were built in 1542 in the time of Henry VIII and long before Elizabeth Castle. They were rebuilt in 1742, abandoned in 1840, then defended again in 1942 by the Germans. The fort is not open to the public and is accessible on foot only at the bottom of the tide – but don't be caught by the incoming flood.

**Railway Walk.** The route of the old railway makes a splendid footpath from St Aubin almost to Corbière, bypassing the tunnel just outside the village. Flowering shrubs line some of the route, and there are plenty of access points.

**Shell House.** But when you drive out of St Aubin on the steep A13, you cannot fail to see Shell House, in truth a bungalow, whose owner has spent more than 30 years building shell-covered terraces in his garden. If you manage to park you are invited to leave a donation for charity.

**NOIRMONT**

At the top of the hill, the B57 branches from the A13 and leads to La Cotte and the little community of Noirmont. A lane past Noirmont Manor goes to Belcroute Bay, the southern extension of St Aubin's Bay, but you can drive on to a car park by the Old Portelet Inn or, passing the obelisk at 209ft (63m) altitude, to a clifftop park 186ft (56m) above the sea.

The view is splendid, covering most of St Aubin's Bay and including Normandy on a clear day. It's no wonder the Germans built a command post here to control the four-storey concrete monstrosity that's now a part of history, as well as nearby gun emplacements. The States bought the headland in 1946 as a memorial to Jersey folk who died as a result of the war, but the Nazi artillery post is seldom open. One of the exhibits by the car park is a 15cm K18 gun that was sited in St Martin, and which the liberating British Army threw over the cliffs by Grosnez Point in February 1946. It was retrieved in June 1979 and sited here. Another gun here was built in Le Havre in 1918.

On the southernmost cliff a little above sea level, *La Tour de Vinde* is a tower built in 1810 at the very high cost of £3,640, to control the approach to St Helier; it takes its name from a clifftop hougue long vanished.

**Janvrin's Tomb.** Portelet Bay has the little high-tide **Ile (Isle) au Guerdain** at its centre, capped by the remains of a Martello-type tower built over the site of Janvrin's grave. Captain Phillipe Janvrin had brought his ship home from Nantes in 1721 with bubonic plague aboard. Refused permission to land, he anchored in Belcroute Bay where he died in quarantine. Still denied the right to come ashore, the body was lowered into its grave on the Ile au Guerdain at a signal from the rector of St Brelade who conducted the funeral service on land. Widow Janvrin moved her husband's remains to St Brelade's cemetery when the risk of disease had gone.

## St BRELADE'S CHURCH

St Brelade's has one of the most picturesque settings of any of the parish churches, standing almost on the seafront and with hills to north and south.

There are two versions of Brelade's origins. Was he Branwalader, probably the son of a 6th-cent Cornish king? Did he study in Wales under St Illtud with a fellow-student called Samson, who took Christianity to Guernsey in 550 and founded St Sampson's church? Did Branwalader therefore, come to Jersey, both men following the Celtic custom of establishing their base on the shoreline as if to spot approaching enemies – or for a quick escape?

*The Fisherman's Chapel stands beside St Brelade's Church.*

Or was he the Irish-born Brendan, more famous for his voyages in the north Atlantic in a flimsy boat? Did he seek shelter here, or was he wrecked?

That first chapel or monastery may have been of wood or stone, but the oldest part of the present church is the foundation of the nave's south wall, built of granite blocks taken from the beach. The north aisle was added in the 13th cent, and extended; the chancel and south porch came in the 14th cent, the tower and west porch in the 15th. By the 16th cent, with the rebuilding of the north aisle and the nave arcade, the church fabric was very much how it looks today, but with Jersey now in the diocese of Winchester, the Reformation brought austere Calvinist beliefs. Out went the altar and the stained glass, as French Protestant refugees came to the island reinforcing Calvinism, with the church gradually changing to Anglican ways only in Victorian times.

**Bell.** In 1551 an Order in Council called for the removal of all bells but one from each parish church, to finance work on Mont Orgueil. Legend says that St Brelade's bells were lost at sea, and can be heard tolling during storms, but the truth is that the present single bell was cast in 1883.

**Brandy.** One would expect a leading producer of French brandy to be a Frenchman, yet Jean Martell was born here, in 1694, and the family seal of a bird and three martels (hammers; the modern French word is *marteaux*), the firm's trade mark as well as the family crest, is in stained glass in the window.

**Fishermen's Chapel.** A tiny chapel stands almost on the cliff edge south of the church, its west and east walls obviously not at a right-angle to the others. It is 43ft (13m) long, externally, by 19ft (6m) wide, with walls 1m thick and 10ft (3m) high. During restoration work in the 1980s it was realised that the raised stone floor covered an earlier floor of beaten clay, and there was evidence of timber post-holes in the ground.

The conclusion is that this chapel not only stands on the site of Branwalader's or Brendan's original church but may, in fact, *be* that church – at least, up to ground level, for the remainder of the walls are definitely Norman, possibly the work of the Bishop of Coutances. If so, the question must be asked: how did it survive the Reformation when virtually all religious guilds and non-essential church buildings were destroyed?

**Armoury.** The answer was known long before the question. Just before the Reformation the chapel became the village armoury, the west wall partly demolished to allow in the parish cannon, which was then aimed out of the east window, over the bay.

It remained the parish armoury until the mid-19th cent after which it became in turn the sexton's store, a carpenter-shop, and a meeting-

*This gun guarding Bel Royal was cast in 1551* for the paryshe of Saynt Peter in Iersse.

room.

A storm in 1818 caused a leak in the roof, which revealed the first of many frescos, now believed to date from around 1315 and which form a major feature of interest, particularly the Annunciation over the restored east window. Another legend claims that the murals change colour as atmospheric humidity varies, so foretelling the coming of a storm – and that's probably why this oldest religious building in Jersey is called the Fishermen's Chapel.

**Perquage and Boot.** A modern stone arch south of the Fishermen's Chapel opens onto the short perquage, a series of steps to the beach, while the road south from the church gate leads to a disused fort, passing Bouilly Port on the way. Search the cliffs here and you may find the grave of Lord Trent, Jesse Boot, the founder of Boots the Chemist. His son gave land around Beau Port, to the west, to the States, which created the Joyce Trent Park.

## JERSEY LAVENDER

On the eastern edge of Le Quennevais, David and Elizabeth Christie have 7 acres (2.8ha) of lavender, planted since 1983 and so forming the second lavender farm in the British Isles, the other being at Heacham, Norfolk – both on sandy soil. From May-Sep, Mon-Sat 1000-1700, visitors stroll the grounds where 55 varieties of *lavandula* grow, forming one of the approved national collections of these plants;

then they watch a video and buy oil, plants, or dried bouquets, all produced here.

There's also a conifer collection, recovering from the hurricane of October 1987, and a 150-year-old gypsy caravan recovering from old age.

**Corbière.** Go west along Route Orange, the A13, then onto B83, and you'll see the specialist nursery of **Geranium Land,** before reaching the old Corbière railway station on the right. At the edge of where the track used to run, stands an enormous oblong lump of red granite, **The Martyr's Table,** or *La Table des Marthes,* brought here by *les p'tits faitiaux,* 'the little people,' who must have had a giant crane or supernatural power to help them. And before 1850, any contract signed or agreement made here by handshake, was considered legally binding.

The **Corbière Lighthouse,** built in 1874, clings to a rock 100ft (30m) above mean sea level, beyond the tip of Corbière Point. You can reach it on foot on the bottom half of the tide – but the flood comes in with great speed, as assistant-keeper Peter Larbalestier discovered when he was drowned on 28 May 1946 trying to save a stranded visitor; a plaque on the causeway tells his story. The headland takes its name from the French *corbeau,* 'raven,' as these large birds have nested here for generations.

The loop road goes back to the A13 then west to La Pulente, where it sweeps around a hairpin bend, offering a splendid view of St Ouen's Bay before plunging down to sea level and the beginning of Five Mile Road to St Ouen.

*A sharp corner on the steep road down to Bonne Nuit Bay.*

# 10: THE NORTH COAST

## Sts Ouen, Mary, John, and Trinity

JERSEY'S NORTH COAST is rugged and beautiful, but there are few points of access and fewer beaches. Despite that, the four northern parishes have plenty to offer, with St Ouen, the largest parish, having more attractions designed purely for the tourist than any other part of the island. Pronounce the name *sa-wen* and you're not far wrong.

## St OUEN

Approaching St Ouen along **Five Mile Road,** which is *four* miles (6.3km) long, you may notice **St Ouen's Pond,** a freshwater lake on the east of the road, and bisected by the parish boundary. For generations this was *La Mare au Seigneur,* the private hunting and fishing ground of the Seigneur of St Ouen. It's now the property of the National Trust for Jersey, which has a birdwatching hide and ringing station on the north shore.

The lowlands from here to L'Etacq Valley, known as **Les Mielles de Morville,** have been listed as a wildlife reserve since 1978, offering protection to overwintering birds as well as to the unusual vegetation, which has yielded more than 400 species on this acidic, peaty soil. The Germans demolished all the houses along this coast and for years after the war it was a rubbish tip. The winds have blown the loose sand to the southern end of the lowlands where the dunes are concentrated.

**St Ouen's Church.** The first side-road north of the pond leads inland to St Ouen's Church, its Norman masonry almost lost in the many extensions and restorations. Its main feature is the central staircase leading to the belfry, a useful vantage point in the days when villagers kept a regular watch for wrecks or invaders.

## St OUEN'S MANOR

The nearby manor house is much more interesting, and is historically the most important on the island as it is the ancestral home of the de Carteret family. It was Philippe de Carteret who recaptured Mont Orgueil from the French in 1468, Helier de Carteret who recolonised Sark for Queen Elizabeth in 1565, and Sir George

Carteret who held the besieged Elizabeth Castle as long as possible during the Civil War.

The family is one of the oldest in the islands, originating in the town of Carteret on the Cotentin peninsula of Normandy and coming to Jersey before the Norman Conquest of England. As a result, of the five *fiefs de la reine* in Jersey, St Ouen has been held the longest by the same family – currently by the 32nd generation, although the direct male descent ended in 1880. The other manors held directly from the Crown are Mélèches, Rozel, Samarès and Trinity, none of which commands a parish.

Samarès Manor in St Clement is the most popular on the island as it is totally commercialised, whereas St Ouen's Manor is open to the public only on rare occasions, although the grounds are open every Tuesday afternoon in summer.

**Castle.** The first record of a building here was in 1135, when it referred to a castle. The oldest surviving part of the structure is the south tower of 1380, while St Anne's Chapel, standing alone in the grounds, is around the same age. The manor's west and north wings are 16th cent, the south and east 17th cent, with further restoration late in the 19th cent. The German Occupation saw the chapel converted into a butcher's shop, which called for further restoration, and rededication, after the war.

In 1941 François Scornet escaped from France in a small boat, but he got no further than Guernsey; a plaque in the grounds recalls his execution by firing squad in the moated and walled grounds of St Ouen's Manor.

Places of interest nearby: the Fantastic Gardens, St Lawrence; the Motor Museum and St Peter's Bunker; La Mare Vineyards and the Jersey Butterfly Farm, St Mary.

## BOUCHET AGATEWARE

North-west of the manor, the village of St Ouen holds the first of the tourist attractions, Bouchet Agateware, in Rue des Marette behind the village hall. Agate is an impure variety of quartz, named from the river Achates in Sicily where it was discovered in Classical times, and Bouchet,claiming to be the world's leading producer of agateware, blends naturally-coloured clays to equal the random bands of hues found in this semi-precious stone. Browse among the selection of small objects, from thimbles and jewellery to delicate handbells.

## JERSEY SHIRE HORSE FARM

The full title adds the word *Museum,* but this is very much a living display of draught horses and other domestic livestock from goats down to rabbits and ducks. The shire horses had to be imported from

*Five geese and the Prince of Wales in Grève de Lecq, with the Paternoster Rocks in the distance.*

England as the final year of the Occupation saw many of the animals killed for meat, after which came the industrial revolution of agriculture. But forget that: marvel at the Shetland pony that can walk erect beneath the belly of a carthorse, let the children enjoy the donkey, and the farrier who demonstrates the shoeing of horses every Wednesday whether he's needed or not. And take a ride in an old Jersey horse-van.

The museum part of the display centres on the collection of horse-powered machinery used on the land for generations, plus a few smaller utensils that relied on manpower. There's also a harness room, play area, gift shop and tea room; the museum is at Champ Donné, by the junction of B34 and C115, open Mar-Oct, Sun-Fri, 1000-1730.

## GREVE DE LECQ

From the village centre the B65 plunges down to the lively hamlet of Grève de Lecq, which owes its popularity to an overlarge free car park as much as to its cliff-ringed beach.

Today's visitors are welcome: there are snack-bars, ice-cream kiosks, the Prince of Wales Hotel and the well-known **Moulin de Lecq,** a watermill whose origins go back to the 14th cent but which has recently been converted to a bar-restaurant of character. It milled its last wheat in 1929, but the stream continues to turn the wooden wheel, which powers the ancient machinery forming an unusual feature

*The Moulin de Lecq, probably the most charming watermill in the island.*

inside the bar. The stream marks the boundary with St Mary parish, which claims a third of the beach as well as the Catel de Lecq; don't bother searching for this Iron Age earthworks as its clifftop ruins are on private land.

But yesterday's visitors were not so welcome. What Iron Age man recognised as a beach vulnerable to invasion, prompted 18th-cent man to defend with an early Martello-type tower, completed in 1780 and now the oldest such fortress in Jersey, standing 35ft (10.5m) high on a 34ft diameter base, and surrounded by parked cars in summer.

## L'ETACQ

The hamlet of L'Etacq, west of the Shire Horse Farm, has a cluster of places of interest, beginning with the **Battle of Flowers Museum** on C114 – but if you come from the south be careful of the very tight hairpin bend. Florence Belchet made her first decorated float in 1934, and went on to establish her reputation by winning many prizes over the years. In 1971 she opened this museum to the Battle of Flowers, and now a dozen of Florence's floats are on permanent display, Mar-Nov daily 1000-1700.

**The Battle of Flowers.** The first battle was in 1902 on Victoria Avenue – the A2 coast road – to mark Edward VII's coronation, and it was an instant success, becoming an annual event except for 1914-18 and 1940-50. Local businessmen revived it in 1951 and the first Miss Battle was elected in 1953, and the event is now the high spot of the tourist season in Jersey, held on an August Thursday amid a week of celebrations.

Several craft shops cluster around the centre of L'Etacq, with a shared car park nearby. The Pottery, Leatherland, and L'Etacq Woodcrafts are workshops that sell their produce at the door; the woodcarvers also have an unusual line in fashioning knife handles and walking-sticks from cabbage stalks. Not just any cabbage – they use the **jersey cabbage,** which can grow 6ft (2m) tall in a season. If you want to try it at home, you can buy seeds here.

## GOLDSMITHS and MICROWORLD

You have a choice of route. The B35 leads south to the top of Five Mile Road, where Jersey Goldsmiths has its showroom at the point where the road bends.

Would you care to see what £1,000,000 in gold bullion looks like? Then step inside – free. The bullion is on display in a reinforced-glass cabinet and looks surprisingly small, no more than would fit into a large holdall. But if it really *is* 24 carat gold, you'd never get away with it as it's 19.32 times heavier than water – a cubic foot weighs 1,206.5lb; a litre, 19.322kg. If you just want to see craftspeople at work on jewellery, that's possible as well. Open year round; Jun-Aug Mon-Fri 1000-2200, Sep-May 1000-1730, plus Sat 1000-1730 all year.

Around the bend and down the straight, Lewis Tower is immediately on the right, its World War Two bunker holding the **Channel Islands Military Museum.** Here are militaria and documents from the British and the German forces, on display daily 1000-1700.

The museum is behind the **Château de Plaisir,** a modern two-storey building holding a night-club and restaurant – and **Micro World,** an incredible exhibition of miniature carvings. Spaniard Manuel Ussa spent years peering through magnifying glasses as he carved his marvellous miniatures. Adam and Eve embrace in a bower – all shaped from the point of a pencil. A minuscule horse balances on the head of a real, but dead, ant. The Sphynx and the Great Pyramid are cut from a single grain of sand, and Tower Bridge balances in the eye of a needle. Ussa had to stop carving every time his heat beat, as the vibration would ruin his work, which is so detailed that visitors have to look through microscopes. Open daily, May-Sep, 1000-1730.

**North.** You *still* have a choice of road. The B35 also leads north-west to a wilder kind of Jersey, where traces of prehistoric man have been found among the rugged cliffs of Le Pinacle. Some authorities claim that Admiral Blake landed his Parliamentarian forces on the beach near L'Etacquerel in 1651, but the amount of reef would need him to come and go at high tide, or to have intimate knowledge of the rocks; other sources place the landing on the open beach in St Peter's parish.

**Grosnez Castle.** North of L'Etacquerel, Les Landes is an area of windswept heath beyond which are the ruins of Grosnez Castle, now little more than a stone archway and the hint of a moat.

This is one of Jersey's enigmas, as nobody knows who built it, why, or when. It's probably early 14th cent. It's probably a defence against repeats of a raid in 1294 when the French killed more than 1,000 islanders; and Bertrand du Guesclin probably destroyed it in another raid in 1373 – or did the English Parliamentarians sack it while besieging Sir George Carteret in Elizabeth Castle? It was certainly destroyed before 1524, as a map drawn that year marks it as a ruin. The name means 'big headland' and is pronounced *gro-nay*.

The B35 swings east to Portinfer hamlet and **Plémont Candlecraft,** the island's only specialist candlemaker. Candles nowadays are for looking at rather than burning; animal-shaped candles are made by pouring suitably-coloured hot wax into a mould and letting it set, but there's more skill in producing carved candles. Take a cold split-mould, pour in hot red wax, then pour it out; pour in orange, and tip the spare out; follow with other colours until you have filled the mould. While the wax is still warm, open the mould, slice down the candle's ribs with a sharp cold knife, and you reveal the rainbow colours. You can try it for yourself here, any day between 0930 and 1730.

Nearby Portinfer Farm has tea rooms where John Wesley's early Methodists used to meet.

And now head north on C105 for **Plémont Holiday Village,** which was originally a Pontins Holiday Camp, built on a 250ft (75m) clifftop. It's breezy, but on perfect days there are splendid views to Guernsey, Sark, Herm and even Alderney, as well as miles of the French coast. A path leads steeply down to the often-deserted beach at **Grève au Lanchon,** or Lançon.

# St MARY

St Mary, the second-smallest parish, has the smallest population. Its **church,** to the west of the village centre, was known in ancient deeds as St Mary of the Burned Monastery, probably recalling a Viking raid. Further tragedy struck in 1042 when Duke William of Normandy ceded a third of the tithes, the church's income, to the Abbey of Cérisy, near Coutances. The tower is now capped with a main steeple and a smaller one at each corner, typically Breton in style but seen in other parts of northern France.

## BUTTERFLIES and GRAPES

Head north-east on C103 to Haute Tombette for the **Jersey Butterfly Centre** which Arthur Rolland created after seeing the large butterflies of Seychelles. The family glasshouses were the first in Jersey to convert to the growing of carnations for bloom, which is still the major source of income, but after seeking the advice of the older Guernsey Butterfly Farm, the Rollands now have Jersey's first walk-in display of *lepidoptera*, the major tourist attraction – unless people come for the tea-room, or the pet tarantula and python. (It's not actually a tarantula, a species which originated in Taranto, Italy; it's more a hairy-legged bird-eating spider from the tropics.) Whatever the attraction, visitors come by the coachload, so drive carefully on the narrow lanes.

**La Mare Vineyards.** The coaches are going on to – or coming from – La Mare Vineyards, almost in sight down C103. In 1969 Robert Blayney established the first vineyard in Jersey for more than a century, and in a video show he explains the difficulties he and the family encountered. The islanders had lost the tradition of growing grapes and producing wine, but the Blayneys, descendants of North Country wine merchants, have succeeded; they also make jams, mustard, and are the island's largest cider pressers – all from this 12-acre (5ha) site more than 300ft (90m) above sea level. Open May-Oct Mon-Sat 1000-1730.

**Devil's Hole.** The coaches don't go the last half mile (1km) to the Devil's Hole, *Le Creux de Vis,* a natural arch that's dangerous to approach too closely as the bottom part of the cliff path is sea-damaged. Some people think *vis* may be a corruption of the Norse word *vik,* an estuary, now found in English as '-wich,' as in 'Ipswich,' but there's only a tiny bay. The 'devil' connection may have come from

*Quetivel Mill, now restored by the Jersey National Trust.*

the prow of a Viking longship, especially if its raiders were responsible for the 'burned monastery,' but it's more likely to be from the figurehead of a ship wrecked here in 1851. The carving should still be here, but it's out of sight from the path.

Nearby: Grève de Lecq and its mill, St Ouen; Fantastic Tropical Gardens, St Peter; Retreat Farm Carnations, St Lawrence; Ronez Point, St John.

# St JOHN

**St John's church,** to the west of the village centre, is named from John the Baptist but its early name was Sanctus Iohannes de Quercubus, inferring there was an oak wood (*quercus* is 'oak') nearby. William de Vauville followed tradition by giving the almost-new church and its income to the Norman Abbey of St Sauveur de Vicompte.

The chancel is original 12th cent, the tower and spire, and the south aisles, being added in the 15th cent. In the 19th cent, members of the congregation wanted to remove a column that blocked the view of the pulpit, but permission was refused in case the church roof fell down as a result. A second appeal was also refused, but when the rector returned from holiday he found part of the column in his garden, and the church roof undamaged.

At the eastern edge of the village, **Jersey Pearl** has a small workshop and sales display, complementing its main shops in Halkett and Broad streets, St Helier.

**Cliffs.** St John's most dramatic appeal is in its cliffs, including **Ronez Point,** the island's northernmost headland. A quarry existed here long before the Occupation, but the Germans found this stone so workable that they laid a railway to Ronez and carved a terrible wound in an otherwise beautiful cliff. The railway has gone, but Ronez Quarry continues to yield granite for numerous building projects. The rock is carried away along the **Route du Nord,** the C100 linking Ronez with St John, which the States built during the war to prevent Jerseymen having to work for the German Army.

The damage is best seen from **Sorel Point** to the west, which has a car park on the headland. Beneath it, the *Lavoir des Dames* is a man-made rock pool, exposed at half-tide. By the way, *sorrel* describes the pinkish granite extracted from Ronez – and *that* name is said to be Norse for 'rocky waste.' How apt!

On the eastern side of St John's Bay, a path plunges 350ft (105m) from a large car park, down the cliffs to **Wolf Caves** and Venus's Bath, both seen only at low tide.

**Bonne Nuit Bay.** Walk a few metres from the car park and you are rewarded by a panoramic view of Bonne Nuit Bay, affording the most sheltered swimming on the north coast. The abandoned fort of La Crête at the eastern headland was built in 1835, but there's nothing at all to see of the Chapel of Sta Maria de Bona Nochte, built in 1150. William de Vauville, who gave St John's church to the Abbey of St Sauveur de Vicompte, also made it a present of the Chapel of St Mary of the Good Night – *Bonne Nuit* in French, which explains the bay's name. But one ancient record lists it as the chapel of the Mala Nochte, the 'bad night.'

The little island in the bay is the ***Cheval de Guillaume,*** 'William's Horse,' another reminder of William de Vauville. In olden times, fishermen would row around the rock on Midsummer Day to ensure good catches for the coming year.

## TRINITY

Sir Edward de Carteret had served Charles II in the role of genteman usher for Black Rod, and he was also Bailiff of Jersey when he died in February 1682. The death occurred in the ancestral manor of St Ouen, but he had instructed in his testament that he should be buried in the vingtaine of Rozel, where he owned a lesser manor with its own chapel and cemetery.

The cortège was driving eastwards to fulfil his wish, when a storm caught the funeral party and scared the horses so badly that the procession was halted near Trinity Church. And there, despite his last request, Sir Edward de Carteret was buried.

*A granite quarry dominates Ronez Point, Jersey's northernmost tip.*

**Trinity Church.** A charter written before 1172 holds the first known reference to the church, when Henry II gave it to the Abbey of St Helier which was later to be incorporated into Elizabeth Castle. The present chancel was built on the site of the original *Chapelle de la Sainte Trinité,* with nave and transepts added to create a ground plan in the form of a cross. The spire, which followed, received a lightning strike in 1629, and *that* prompted the comment that it was a sign of God's displeasure at 'the pontifical grandeur of the Dean.'

Trinity **Manor,** south-west of the village centre, was a Tudor building that hosted the future Charles II in 1646 while his father was desperately trying to cling to the throne. The manor was in ruins by 1910, when a three-year restoration gave it the appearance of a French château. It is not open to the public.

## JERSEY ZOO

Trinity's main attraction is known around the world for its work on animal conservation and rehabilitation: Jersey Zoo, in the grounds of Les Augrès Manor, the property of author and broadcaster Gerald Durrell – his main home is in the south of France. Zoos in general are coming under criticism for their habit of treating animals purely as exhibits, but Durrell's aim was to save breeding stock of species that were in danger of extinction in the wild; this meant he had to replicate their natural environment and avoid the problem of boredom. The **Jersey Wildlife Preservation Trust** has no concrete terraces, no

*The splendid gardens of Shell House, St Aubin, one man's contribution to Jersey's charm.*

chimps' tea parties, and does not take animals purely because they are what one would expect in a zoo. So don't look for elephants or giraffes.

Instead, you'll probably find golden lion tamarins and marmosets, water dragons and Bali starlings, lemurs and snow leopards, red-footed tortoises and orang-utans, some of which have been re-established in their native habitats.

Readers of *My Family and Other Animals* will recall that Durrell was an avid collector as a child, but he met major difficulties when trying to establish a zoo with conservation overtones. Finally, his publisher Rupert Hart-Davis agreed to guarantee a loan of £25,000, and introduced him to Major Hugh Fraser who wanted to sell the 16th-cent Les Augrès Manor and return to England. Durrell rented it, with the option of purchase, and early in 1959 Jersey Zoo opened on this 30-acre (12-ha) site.

Statues of dodos stand on the pillars by the entrance from the car park, and the symbol is repeated throughout the public buildings, which include the new Princess Royal Pavilion holding the activity centre, as well as the gift shop in the visitor centre, and a café. Open daily (excl 25 Dec) 1000-1800 or dusk if earlier.

## ORCHID FOUNDATION

South of the zoo, but with better access from the A8, the collecting and conservation theme continues at the Eric Young Orchid Foundation in Victoria Village. Young settled in Jersey after the war and began his orchid collection in 1958, adding to it the stock of a nursery that was closing. By the 1970s, after he had propagated several varieties, his orchids were rated as the finest such collection in Europe, but he died before finding a suitable location to put them on permanent public display. The purpose-built glasshouses at Victoria Village have now fulfilled that dream, and Mr Young's collection is open year-round Thur-Sat (ex bank hols), 1000-1600.

## HERITAGE STEAM MUSEUM

Lyndon Pallot was another collector and conservationist, but with a difference. He began his working life as a trainee engineer on the Jersey Railway, based at the old Weighbridge (now Liberation Sq) in St Helier. He moved on to become an agricultural engineer, carrying his love of steam engines into another field – in two senses.

His passion for collecting led him to save many steam-powered engines which now form the basis of the the biggest inanimate tourist attraction in the parish, the Pallot Heritage Steam Museum in Rue de Bechet, open Apr-Oct Mon-Sat 1000-1700. It's a privately-owned collection of mobile and static engines that spent their working lives on farms, roadbuilding jobs, or railways, and which caught Mr Pallot's eye before it was too late. There's a Merlin portable steam engine built in 1924 – it's on wheels, but can't move under its own power – a Ransomes traction engine built in Ipswich in 1904, a static Tangye engine from 1898, and others.

**Railway.** The biggest as well as the most important attraction is undoubtedly *La Meuse,* an 0-6-0 standard-gauge steam locomotive which hauls two Victorian carriages along a short section of track on Liberation Day and other special occasions – but there's usually one engine under steam every opening day. Almost as an afterthought, there is a 2ft-gauge (60cm) railway as well as some ancient kitchen appliances.

Trinity's coast has the beautiful **Bouley Bay** at its centre, with some splendid views from the C102 which snakes down the cliff-face to the sands. As there's no village around the tiny jetty, the British Hill Climbing Association gets permission to close the road for its annual championships, fought out on almost any kind of wheeled vehicle.

**Rozel.** Rozel is a hamlet huddled around the beautiful Rozel Bay – and parking is difficult. In the early 20th cent it was a tiny fishing community, with army barracks built in 1809; they are now part of Le Couperon Hotel.

**Botanist.** The botanist Samuel William Curtis who lived here in the 19th cent planted numerous trees and shrubs on the south-facing slope of Rozel valley, his handkerchief tree a splendid sight in May.

The name Rozel comes from the French *rousseau,* an archaic word for 'red,' and was bestowed on the community by a seigneur from Normandy who owned land here. The Lord of the Manor of Rozel, and the Lord of Les Augrès Manor, currently Gerald Durrell, share the honour of being Royal Butlers, which gives them status during a royal visit to the island. And the manor, home of the Lemprière family since 1360 except for several gaps, is where Sir Edward de Carteret wanted to be buried in 1682. Don't look for it in Trinity; it's deep in the parish of St Martin.

# 11: THE EAST COAST

## Sts Martin, Clement, Savoir – and Grouville

JERSEY'S EAST COAST loses its cliffs at Mont Orgueil, the island's most easterly point, and from there to Havre des Pas on the fringe of St Helier, aeons of winds and tides have deposited their sands making a low-lying coastal plain. Between high- and low-water marks there is one continuous stretch of sand, but where it sweeps around Plat Rocque Point it leaves acres of granite boulders exposed at low tide.

The biggest magnet by far for tourists is the impressive Mont Orgueil, but visitors shouldn't miss the Hougie Bie, Samarès Manor, and Lillie Langtry's bust in the churchyard of St Saviour, the only parish without a coastline.

## St MARTIN

### MONT ORGUEIL, Gorey Castle

When Henry II died in 1189, his personal realms stretched from the Cheviots to the Pyrenees and he had control over Scotland (excluding the Hebrides and northern isles which were Norwegian), Ireland, and the remainder of Wales from his maternal inheritance. South of the Channel he held Maine, Anjou and Touraine as direct monarch, and Normandy, Brittany, Aquitaine, Gascony and Auvergne through his marriages and treaties. In effect, he ruled from Cape Wrath to Lourdes, from Limerick almost to the Rhône Valley – excluding only the Isle of Man.

John became King of England 10 years later with much the same territory under his control. But Philippe II of France snatched back Normandy, and soon John had lost all his continental possessions except Aquitaine and Gascony, the latter staying with England until 1453.

**'Lackland.'** John, who by 1204 had earned the soubriquet 'Lackland,' nearly lost the Channel Islands to France, and decided that sturdy defences were needed to prevent any invasion – and in the next four centuries France was to make 15 attempts.

Work began that same year on Gorey Castle, crowning a prominence which controlled the northern end of the long beach. The castle was planned as a series of concentric defences whose mid-point was the **Keep,** holding the Great Hall and kitchen. The **Middle Ward** followed, occupying slightly lower ground to the south, with the **Lower Ward** at the southern end. It was, and still is, a formidable bastion and until Elizabeth Castle superceded it, Jersey could not fall to any invader as long as Gorey Castle held out.

The first attack had come in 1214, but was repulsed. In 1338 the French Admiral Nicholas Behuchet invaded Jersey but retired when he failed to seize Gorey Castle; the next year a fleet of 52 ships also failed, and another land-based assault in 1374 was equally unsuccessful. Bertrand du Guesclin, Connétable of France, seized the island in a surprise attack in 1364, but once again Gorey Castle held out.

**Mont Orgueil** Much later, the Duke of Clarence, brother of Henry V (1413-'22), was so impressed by Gorey Castle's impregnability that he renamed it Mont Orgueil, 'Mount Pride.' But ignominious surrender was near, for Edward IV's queen, Margaret of Anjou, became a traitor to her husband's cause when she *gave* the Channel Islands to her cousin, the Grand Sénéschal of France, in 1461. It was the only time the French set foot in Mont Orgueil as rulers, and then only for an occupation of seven years. In 1468 Philippe de Carteret besieged the castle by land while Sir Richard Harliston blockaded it from the sea for five months, the two ultimately managing to regain Mount Pride.

There's an interesting anecdote to this story in that Thomas de Havilland, who helped Philippe de Carteret, was an ancestor of film actresses Joan Fontaine and Olivia de Havilland.

*Gorey harbour at low tide. The railway once ran along the promenade, and passenger ferries sailed to France.*

Mont Orgueil lost its military supremacy when cannons replaced bows and arrows. Quite quickly, the nearby Mont St Nicholas, now topped by the Victoria Tower, became an ideal spot to mount heavy artillery, which could then fire down into the unprotected wards of the castle. Mont Orgueil was finished: long live Elizabeth Castle!

Sir Walter Raleigh opposed plans to demolish the castle for building stone, and so Mont Orgueil's role in subsequent history was as a prison, its most notable inmates being Sir William Prynne the seditious libeller of Charles I and, soon after, Dean Bandinel and his son who tried to escape by the then new idea of making a rope from knotted bedsheets. They failed. The castle was a temporary refuge for aristocratic refugees during the French Revolution, with Admiral Philippe d'Auvergne leading his Royalist counter-operation from here. That failed as well.

Britain handed the castle to the States of Jersey before the First World War, and the Germans added gun posts, observation towers and a flame-thrower during the Second War.

## MONT ORGUEIL TODAY

The easiest way to tour the castle is to enter at the north-west corner, the **First Gate,** from the B29 road above the town. From here, by the **Harliston Tower** built in 1470, the only serious climb is from the entrance kiosk at the **Second Gate** by the Lower Ward, up to the Keep, with the option of turning away and taking the long descent to the waterfront.

The **Lower Ward**'s Southern Tower commands a good view out to sea, and from the ward's northern wall a series of steps takes you through the **Third Gate,** renamed Queen's Gate after Victoria's visit in 1846. **St George's Tower** on your left guards the Lower Ward as the steps turn sharply right for the **Fourth Gate,** now Queen Elizabeth's Gate – the first queen, not the second. On your left the **Round Tower** overlooks the entrance, but much of the **Middle Ward** on your right is in ruins. Across the open space, **St George's Crypt** holds the remains of governors Thomas Overay, buried in 1500, and Sir Anthony Ughtred who died in 1532.

The massive **Somerset Tower,** built in 1680 by Edward Seymour, later Duke of Somerset, was the last major work on the castle, to allow cannon to bear on the menacing hillside opposite, but the masonry was so thick that there was room for only two demi-culverins, which are small cannon, with two others aimed towards Jeffrey's Leap. Nowhere else in the heart of the castle is strong enough to withstand artillery.

John de Roches, 14th cent Keeper of the Castle, contributed **Rochefort Tower** to the north, from where there is a small sally port (in Spanish, a *puerta de salir,* an 'exit-door'), now in ruins.

One of René Lalique's angels guards the door to the Glass Church.

**Tableaux.** At the centre of the original castle, several rooms contain lifesize wax tableaux showing important events in the castle's history: 1373, and du Guesclin's attack; the Poulette family who governed the island from this castle; Admiral Philippe d'Auvergne in his Chair of Office; and some of the famous prisoners held here. A passage leads to Prynne's Tower where the libeller was held.

**Jeffrey's Leap.** Around the headland north of Gorey, a rugged headland offers a good view across Anne Port. It was from this spot that criminals in Medieval times were forced to jump onto the rocks beneath, bound hand and foot. Legend claims that a certain Jeffrey survived the leap uninjured and was therefore free – but he tried it again and killed himself. History is more prosaic, stating that Jeffrey, or Geoffroy, was convicted of a second crime and chose this punishment, hoping to escape again. He didn't.

**Dolmen de Faldouet.** Inland a little, the 2,500-year-old Dolmen de Faldouet, also called *La Pouquelaye de Faldouet,* is a well-preserved passage-grave 50ft (15m) long, with one of its capping stones estimated to weight 24 tons. When excavated in 1839, remains of adults and children were found, with several grave offerings now in the Jersey Museum.

**Archirondel Tower.** The Archirondel Tower, built in 1794, was one of the chain of forts built around the coast against a threatened invasion from France. They are all called Martello towers although they predate the English towers of bolder design, which were based on the original tower in Mortella. But Archirondel was different. Not only did it, and La Rocco in St Ouen's Bay, have curtain walls, but Archirondel was planned as the southern defence of a great naval harbour to be built in St Catherine's Bay to counter the menace from the new harbour at Cherbourg. **St Catherine's Breakwater** was to be the northern arm of the harbour but after it was finished in 1855 the idea was abandoned in favour of Saye Bay, Alderney, protected by a giant breakwater. It couldn't withstand the Atlantic storms, and Britain's final answer to Cherbourg was Portland Harbour.

**St Martin's Church.** Martin was a bishop of Tours who had sent missionaries out into the wilds of north-western France; a third of Normandy's churches are dedicated to St Martin, and both Guernsey and Jersey have parishes bearing his name.

This church was mentioned in 1042 when Duke William of Normandy gave it to the Abbey of Cérisy near Coutances, with a third of its tithe of grain; it was common practise at the time to rob the island of its produce.

The Abbot of Cérisy appointed the rectors of St Martin until the Reformation, when the church was gutted and abandoned, but its steeple, although a mile inland, served as a lighthouse to local shipping when the Spanish Armada was coming up-channel.

Records show that the last man to use St Martin's *perquage* was Thomas le Seeleur who escaped the gallows in 1546.

## GOREY

If the word 'charming' can apply to anywhere in Jersey, then it must describe Gorey, a small town nestling under the protective bulk of Mont Orgueil, which is accessible by steps from the quayside. The jetty was built in 1820 and extended in 1826, but there must have been something there already as Gorey is described as having 'the most ancient harbour' and is, with St Helier, the only official port.

Nothing remains of the Jersey Eastern Railway which came here from St Helier, but the harbourside car park is on the site of the station, and flower gardens grow where the trains once ran.

**Jersey Diamond.** Would you like to see the Koh-i-Noor Diamond? You can't, as it's in the Crown Jewels – but Jersey Diamond, overlooking Gorey Pier, has copies of many famous stones and is the island's leading gemmologist. It is also involved in the Living Legend.

**Jersey Pottery.** Pottery is much more mundane than diamonds, but the workshops of Jersey Pottery draw large crowds to Gorey Village, across the parish boundary in Grouville. The business began in the early 1950s with 12 people, and now has around 70 on the payroll, producing a range of around 200 items of merchandise including unlikely objects such as picture frames and clock cases, in an equally wide price range.

*An ancient millstone is re-erected in the grounds of the Hougue Bie.*

There are no guided tours, but visitors are free to wander around and see the potters at work year-round Mon-Fri 0900-1730, except bank hols. The shop now has a garden restaurant with the same opening hours, and there's a pottery shop at 1 Bond St, St Helier.

# GROUVILLE

The ancient church of St Martin de Grouville is on the A3, in the community of La Fontaine and the vingtaine of La Rue. According to a charter from Duke Robert of Normandy it was serving the parish in 1035 although the nave is supposedly 10th cent. One Godefroi de Buisson gave the church and all its tithes to the Abbey of the Holy Trinity at Lessay, north of Coutances, in 1149, and the Bishop of Coutances appointed the rectors until 1568, by which time the church had suffered the depredations of the Reformation. Today's font was part of St Helier's Town Church until the Reformation, and it served as a pig trough before being rescued for Grouville Church.

## HOUGUE BIE

Grouville's most important site, for archaeologists as well as for coach parties, is the Hougue Bie, a museum of ancient and modern history, and of legend.

The legend is simple. After the Lady of Hambye learned that her Lord had slain the dragon of Goose Green Marsh (see chapter 5) and had in turn been killed by his servant, she came to Jersey and ordered a great mound of earth to be built over her husband's grave: it certainly gives this 40ft (13m) hillock its name, and acknowledges that it was man-made.

The truth is that the mound is around 5,000 years old, covering a Neolithic passage-grave 72ft (22m) long, with several enormous capping stones, one estimated to weigh 25 tons. The chamber was virtually empty when excavated in 1924, but a few tiny artefacts such as beads and pot shards were found.

**Fact or fiction?** Legend claims that Lady Hambye built a chapel on top of the mound, to be visible from her home in Normandy. In truth, the chapel of *Nôtre Dame de la Clarté,* 'Our Lady of Light,' was built on top around the 12th cent; it is 20ft (6.2m) long. And in the 16th cent Dean Mabon built another chapel to commemorate his safe return from a pilgrimage to Jerusalem; its crypt has a copy of the Holy Sepulchre and it incorporated Lady Hambye's chapel under its own roof.

**Tower.** And then came Major-General James d'Auvergne, who bought the Hougue Bie in 1759 and in 1780 built a tower over the chapels, in order to relay messages by semaphore or flags between Mont Orgueil and Elizabeth Castle. The tower was demolished in 1924 as a hazard; days later the workmen cut into the base of the

*There's a long, long trail a-winding from Elizabeth Castle to the town.*

*St Catherine's Breakwater offers shelter to small boats, but originally the British fleet was to anchor here.*

mound and found the passage-grave.

**Museums.** But there's more to the Hougue Bie than just this mound. The Agricultural Museum has a display of farm machinery from the 19th cent onwards, outside which is a cluster of staddle stones, looking like giant mushrooms but used for supporting stooks of corn. A stook? Before combine harvesters were invented, an armful of cut corn was a *sheaf*, twelve of which stacked together made *stook* or *shock*.

The Geological Museum has rock samples from the island, starting with shale, at 700,000,000 years, the oldest. The Archaeological Room looks from Palaeolithic man to the brief Roman incursion, and the Occupation Museum specialises in the 9-ft (2.7m) rowing boat that **Denis Vibert** used in his escape from St Aubin's Bay in 1941. Three nights later a British destroyer picked him up on the edge of a minefield near Portland Bill. He was the only islander to escape.

# St SAVIOUR

Think of St Saviour and you think of Lillie Langtry, whose story is told in chapter 7 and whose marble monument stands in the cemetery of St Saviour's Church.

The church had a strange beginning. Four families each built a chapel: St Jean in the north-east, St Sauveur de l'Epine in the east, La Sainte Vierge Marie in the west and another St Martin in the north-west, each having its own priest.

The chapels of the Holy Saviour and the Holy Virgin Mary were joined before 1145, when the name of St Saviour first appears in records; the other chapels were integrated in the 14th cent. In 1563, when the Black Death struck Jersey, the Royal Court left little St Helier and met in this church.

## St CLEMENT

Victor Hugo was St Clement's most illustrious inhabitant, until his outburst against Queen Victoria in *L'Homme* newspaper prompted the Lieutenant-Governor to deport him. The Connétable of St Clement had the duty of escorting Hugo to St Helier port, from where he sailed to Guernsey.

**Church.** A 17th-cent rector, François Valpy, had his own encounter with the law when he prosecuted the Seigneur of Samarès for altering a manorial pew without permission. The seigneur responded by filling another of his pews with his servants, barring Valpy's access to the pulpit.

Restoration in 1879 exposed numerous 15th-cent frescos in the nave. On the north wall, St Michael fights the dragon; on the west wall of the south transept an old French poem tells a hunting story; and the north transept has St Barbara of Heliopolis losing her head for her beliefs.

*The grounds of Samares Manor in St Clement are open to the public.*

# SAMARES MANOR

The smallest and southernmost of Jersey's parishes has the busiest manor house, **Samarès Manor,** built on the edge of the *salse marais,* the salt-marsh which gave it its name. The land between the manor and Le Nez Point is below high-tide and was often used as salt-pans, allowing the sun to evaporate sea-water and so yield the precious mineral. The last major flood in 1811 urged the States to build a sea wall beside which the A4 road now runs.

**Samarès Manor** has gone into the stately homes business in a big way, landscaping much of its 14 acres (5.6ha) of grounds and offering guided tours of the saffron-yellow house, known particularly for its drawing room in the style of William and Mary. The cost of improving the gardens in 1924 was the monstrous sum of £100,000 and the labour of 40 gardeners, but the result was the accolade of the most beautiful house in the British realm.

You can see it now, Apr-Oct, daily, 1000-1700 (house tours 1030, 1115, 1200), the large car park and good bus service making excuses futile.

The main points of interest begin with the 11th-cent dove cote or *colombier* inside the gate. This is the oldest dove cote in Jersey and is a circular roofless tower with nesting-places on the inside of the walls for 500 birds. In Medieval times the doves or pigeons yielded a useful crop of eggs, and the birds themselves were fresh meat for lean days in winter.

Black swans live on the pond dug in 1924, and the Japanese-style pagoda and summerhouse were added in 1930. The herb garden and walled garden produce more than 500 varieties and species, many of them on sale in the nursery shop – and the children enjoy rides in a horse-drawn Jersey-style farm wagon.

The Farmyard is a large open square surrounded by outbuildings where you can see many aspects of bygone farm life: early 20th-cent tools, old motor vehicles, women spinning and weaving, men making toys, the itinerant farrier...it's the olden days brought back to life.

## AND FINALLY..

The **Dolmen of Mont Ubé,** 200m east of Samarès Manor, is a Neolithic passage-grave discovered in 1848 and estimated to be 4,000 years old; it is notable as being the only ancient site where cremated and uncremated remains have been found side by side. Even the tiny **Green Island,** also known as La Motte, 200m south of Jersey's southernmost tip, was used as a cemetery in prehistoric times, as 18 graves were discovered in 1911.

As you stand on the slipway between Le Croc and Le Nez Point and watch the high tide cover the sands, it is easy to think of the tides of humanity that have flooded these islands, beginning with Stone Age man, followed by Roman, Viking, Celt, Norman, English, German, and finally tourists from all over the world. But at this moment there is nobody in the entire British Channel Islands further south than *you* – unless it's somebody on the Minkies reef.

## THE SMALLER ISLANDS

**Les Minquiers.** Absolutely the most southerly part of the *British* Channel Islands, these reefs lie due south of Jersey and half way to St Malo. Popularly known as 'The Minquies,' this treacherous group of rocks was decreed to be British territory at The Hague in 1953 after the French claimed it to be a dependency of the Chausey Islands. This reef and Les Ecréhous have permanent houses on them.

**Les Ecréhous.** North-east of Jersey and almost half way to Carteret lie Les Ecréhous, a few tiny islands on a dangerous reef; on a clear day at low tide they're just visible from Jersey. In 1961 Jerseyman Alphonse le Gastelois took up permanent residence in the islands where he stayed for 14 years, but Phillipe Pinel, also from Jersey, lived here from 1848 to 1892 and became known as the 'King of the Ecréhous.' The reef has long been accepted as part of St Martin's parish, Jersey, but the French challenged tradition at the International Court of Justice at The Hague in 1953 and claimed it. The court decided it was British territory.

**Les Casquets.** The Casquets reef 5 miles (8km) west of Alderney has wrecked many ships, including the *Blanch Nef* in 1120, in which Henry I's only legitimate son, William, drowned. The first lighthouse, built in 1726, had a coal fire; later lights were St Peter, St Thomas and Donjon, on the highest rock which reaches 100ft (30m) above sea level.

**Les Roches Douvres.** These uninhabited rocks lie 20 miles (32km) west of Jersey. This was where Denis Vibert was driven ashore on his first attempt to escape from Jersey in World War Two.

**Les Iles Chausey.** Midway between the Minkies and Granville, the Chausey Isles were returned to French rule at the Peace of Aix-la-Chapelle in 1668. The main land is Grande Ile, holding the tiny village of Blainvillais, a fort of 1866 and another built in 1928 for Louis Renault the car manufacturer. There are also a church, lighthouse, school, shop, and several hotels, reached by small boat from Granville; around 50 islets remain at high tide, with vast reefs exposed at low water.

The Chausey Isles issued their own postage stamps in 1961 until the French Government suppressed them in 1963, six years after Herm's postal service was withdrawn. Living on a tiny island certainly creates an air of independence – could the larger islands be a little bit envious?

# 12: WHEN THE SUN GOES DOWN

## Where to stay in Jersey

JERSEY PIONEERED THE HOTEL GRADING SYSTEM, and now inspects all premises with more than five bedrooms, classifying them with sun symbols ranging from five down to one. Guest houses, too numerous to list here, are graded with diamonds, three to one. The most expensive is probably the Little Grove in St Lawrence, at more than £100 per person per day, high season, with the least expensive asking less than £20; you can probably get down to £15 in low season, with all prices based on two sharing. Guernsey has dearer and cheaper hotels.

**Symbols.** The symbols show ⋈ the number of bedrooms; ✗ if there is a restaurant on the premises; ♀ if there is a licensed bar; ♿ whether disabled guests are accepted (usually by appointment); ↴ if there is a pool, indoor or outdoor.

The information given here should be taken as approximate, as it is subject to change. For more information, contact Jersey Tourism at Liberation Square, St Helier, JE1 1BB, ✆24779, or for reservations ✆31958; or contact your travel agent or tour operator.

**Addresses.** Letters in the address indicate the parish, viz:

| | | | |
|---|---|---|---|
| B | St Brelade | Mn | St Martin |
| C | St Clement | My | St Mary |
| G | Grouville | O | St Ouen |
| H | St Helier | P | St Peter |
| J | St John | S | St Saviour |
| L | St Lawrence | T | Trinity |

## 5-SUN HOTEL
Longueville Manor, S, ⋈32✗, ♀, ↴.

## 4-SUN HOTELS
**Atlantic,** La Moye, B, ⋈50✗, ♀, ↴; **Chateau la Chaire,** Rozel, Mn, ⋈13✗, ♀; **Grand,** Esplanade, H, ⋈116✗, ♀, ↴; **Horizon,** L' ⋈104✗, ♀, ↴; **St Brelade's Bay,** B, ⋈72, ♀, ♿.

## 3-SUN HOTELS

Ambassadeur, C, ⋈41✕, Ω, ⌐; Arches, Les, Archirondel, M, ⋈54, Ω, ⌐; Apollo, H, ⋈85, Ω, ⌐; Beaufort, H, ⋈54, Ω, ⌐; Beau Rivage, B, ⋈27, Ω; Beausite, G, ⋈76, Ω, ⌐; Bergerac, Portelet Bay, B, ⋈43, Ω, ⌐; Chalet, Le, Corbière, B, ⋈25✕, Ω, ⌐; Chateau Valeuse, B, ⋈33✕, Ω, ⌐; Cheval Roc, Bonne Nuit Bay, J, ⋈42, Ω, ⌐; Couperon de Rozel, Le, M, ⋈35✕, Ω, ♿, ⌐; Cristina, L, ⋈60✕, Ω, ⌐; Emeraude, L' S, ⋈58, Ω, ⌐; Fort d'Auvergne, Havre des Pas, H, ⋈65, Ω; France, De, S, ⋈321, Ω, ⌐.

Grouville Bay, G, ⋈56, Ω, ⌐; Place, La, B, ⋈40✕, Ω, ♿, ⌐; Plage, De La, Havre des Pas, H, ⋈78, Ω, ⌐; Laurels, H, ⋈37, Ω, ♿, ⌐; Little Grove, L, ⋈13✕, Ω, ♿; Lobster Pot, L'Etacq, O, ⋈13✕, Ω; Mermaid, P, ⋈68✕, Ω, ⌐; Moorings, Gorey, M, ⋈16✕, Ω; Mount View, H, ⋈35, Ω; Old Court House, Gorey, G, ⋈58, Ω, ♿, ⌐; Ommaroo, Havre des Pas, H, ⋈85, Ω; Pomme d'Or, H, ⋈150✕, Ω; Portelet, B, ⋈86⋈✕, ⌐; Revere, H, ⋈44✕, Ω, ⌐; Rex, H, ⋈53, Ω, ⌐; Royal, H, ⋈88✕, Ω; Royal Yacht, ⋈44✕, Ω; Samarès Coast, C, ⋈52, Ω, ⌐; Sarum, H, ⋈49, Ω; Savoy, H, ⋈61✕, Ω, ⌐; Sea Crest, B, ⋈7✕, Ω, ⌐; Shakespeare, C, ⋈32✕, Ω; Silver Springs, B, ⋈88, Ω, ⌐; Somerville, B, ⋈59✕, Ω, ♿, ⌐; Uplands, H, ⋈43, Ω, ⌐; Washington, H, ⋈36, Ω, ⌐; Water's Edge, Bouley Bay, T, ⋈51✕, Ω, ⌐;

## 2-SUN HOTELS

Alexandra, H, ⋈57, Ω; Alhambra, H, ⋈16✕, Ω; Almorah, H, ⋈14, Ω; Allandale, H, ⋈16✕, Ω, ⌐; Alton, H, ⋈36, Ω, ♿; Angleterre, H, ⋈92, Ω; Bay View, H, ⋈41, Ω; Berkshire, H, ⋈65, Ω; Biarritz, B, ⋈67; Blenheim, L, ⋈35, Ω, ⌐; Cambrai, P, ⋈33, Ω, ⌐; Carlton, Havre des Pas, H, ⋈48, Ω; Central, H, ⋈72, Ω; Charrière, Les, P, ⋈41✕, Ω, ⌐; Château de la Mer, Havre des Pas, H, ⋈5✕, Ω; Chelsea, H, ⋈114, Ω, ⌐; Cliff Court, H, ⋈16, Ω, ⌐; Coralie, L, ⋈53, Ω; Cornucopia, H, ⋈15✕, Ω, ⌐; Côte du Nord, T, ⋈12✕; Dolphin, Gorey, M, ⋈16✕, Ω; Fontaine, La, C, ⋈20, Ω, ⌐; Golden Sands, B, ⋈50, Ω; Graham, H, ⋈27, Ω, ⌐; Grange Court, H, ⋈27, Ω; Green Hill, P, ⋈18✕, Ω.

Hampshire, H, ⋈47, Ω, ♿, ⌐; Hermitage, L' P, ⋈119, Ω, ⌐; Highfield, T, ⋈25, Ω, ⌐; Highlands, Corbière, B, ⋈56, ♿, ⌐; Idlerocks, Bonne Nuit Bay, J, ⋈13, Ω, ⌐; Haule Manoir, La, B, ⋈20✕, Ω; Lavender Villa, G, ⋈21, Ω, ⌐; Leighton, H, ⋈35, Ω; Magnolia, L, ⋈21✕, Ω; Maison Gorey, Gorey, G, ⋈30✕, Ω; Marina, Havre des Pas, H, ⋈37, Ω; Mayfair, H, ⋈161, Ω, ♿, ⌐; Merton, S, ⋈330, Ω, ⌐; Metropole, H, ⋈137, Ω, ⌐; Millbrook House, H, ⋈24, Ω; Miramar, B, ⋈38, Ω; Mont de la Rocque, St Aubin, B, ⋈24, Ω; Monterey, H, ⋈72, Ω, ⌐; Mont Félard, L, ⋈18✕, Ω; Mont Millais, H, ⋈44✕, Ω, ⌐; Mornington, H, ⋈31, Ω; Norfolk Lodge, H, ⋈106, Ω, ⌐; Normandie, De, Havre de Pas, H, ⋈106, Ω, ♿, ⌐; Oaklands Lodge, T, ⋈10✕, Ω; Oasis, L' G, ⋈41, Ω; Old Bank House, Gorey, M, ⋈20, Ω; Old Court House, St Aubin, B, ⋈9✕, Ω, ⌐; Pontac House, C, ⋈27, Ω, ⌐; Portland, H, ⋈72, Ω, ⌐; Queen's, H, ⋈37, Ω.

Raleigh, H, ⋈27, Ω, ⌐; Rondel, La, Archirondel, M, ⋈22✕, Ω, ⌐; Rosebank, H, ⋈48, Ω, ⌐; Royal Bay, Gorey, G, ⋈16, Ω; Runnymede Court, H, ⋈57, Ω; St Aubyn, St Aubin, B, ⋈19✕; St Clement's Bay, C, ⋈47✕, Ω; Sandranne, H, ⋈31, Ω; Sandringham,0 H, ⋈38, Ω, ♿; Stafford, H, ⋈37, Ω; Swansons, H, ⋈37, Ω; Talana, S, ⋈41, Ω, ⌐; Tour, La, St Aubin, B, ⋈21✕, Ω; Trafalgar Bay, Gorey, G, ⋈27, Ω, ♿, ⌐; Vauvert, H, ⋈19, Ω; Westhill, H, ⋈90, Ω, ⌐; West View, My, ⋈33, Ω, ⌐; White Heather, L, ⋈33, Ω, ⌐; Willows, S, ⋈24, Ω; Windmills, B, ⋈38✕, Ω, ⌐; Woodville, H, ⋈62, Ω, ⌐.

## 1-SUN HOTELS

Bantry House, H, ⋈33, Ω, ⌐; Barra, H, ⋈68, Ω; Beach, Gorey, M, ⋈37, Ω; Beachcombers, G, ⋈44, Ω, ⌐; Belle Plage, C, ⋈20, Ω, ⌐; Bon Air, C, ⋈19, Ω, ⌐; Bonne Nuit, Bonne Nuit Bay, J, ⋈30✕, Ω; Clarence, H, ⋈44, Ω; Coie, Le, H, ⋈197, Ω, ⌐; Colesberg, H, ⋈33, Ω; Corona, H, ⋈19, Ω; Creux, Les, B, ⋈26, Ω.

Glenthorne, H, ◄18, ♀; Greenwood Lodge, H, ◄33, ♀; Grève de Lecq, Grève de Lecq, M, ◄23, ♀; Kalamunda, Gorey, G, ◄28, ♀, 🔥; Leoville, O, ◄31, ♀, ⚡; Mandalay, H, ◄41, ♀; Monaco, H, ◄36, ♀, 🔥; Mont St Clair, S, ◄36, ♀; Newton, St Aubin, B, ◄18, ♀; Oakbey, H, ◄30, ♀; Ocean, H, ◄52, ♀, 🔥; Puits, Du, O, ◄14✖, ♀, ⚡; Santa Monica, H, ◄30, ♀; Suisse, H, ◄36, ♀.

## GUEST HOUSES

Jersey has around 150 guest houses, the largest being Leofric Lodge in St Saviour, and Palms in St Helier, each with 24 rooms; the smallest the three-room Avenues Farm in Trinity. Prices, per person (assuming two sharing) per night, can reach single figures, or rise to the mid-twenties in pounds.

## OTHER ACCOMMODATION

The **Self-catering** properties include hotels, guest-houses, and private houses, and are invariably let by the week. The **holiday villages,** Jersey Village at Portelet Bay and Pontins at Plémont, have 121 and 200 rooms respectively, and there are **campsites** at Beuveland (St Martin); Quennevais, Rose Farm, and St Brelade's Camping Park all in St Brelade; Summer Lodge at Léoville, St Ouen; and at Rozel.

*The beautiful north coast has the odd pocket of farmland. Bonne Nuit Bay is in the distance.*

# INDEX